DEVIL'S
ADVOCATES:
The Unnatural History of Lawyers

BY ANDREW ROTH
&
JONATHAN ROTH

Edited by Barbara Repa
Illustrated by Gordon Grabe

Nolo Press • 950 Parker St., Berkeley, CA 94710

IMPORTANT

Nolo Press is committed to keeping its books up-to-date. Each new printing, whether or not it is called a new edition, has been revised to reflect the latest law changes. This book was printed and updated on the last date indicated below. Before you rely on information in it, you might wish to call Nolo Press (415) 549-1976 to check whether a later printing or edition has been issued.

PRINTING HISTORY

New "**Printing**" means there have been some minor changes, but usually not enough so that people will need to trade in or discard an earlier printing of the same edition. Obviously, this is a judgment call and any change, no matter how minor, might affect you.

New "**Edition**" means one or more major, or a number of minor, law changes since the previous edition.

FIRST EDITION	July 1989
ILLUSTRATIONS	Gordon Grabe
PRODUCTION	Stephanie Harolde
BOOK DESIGN & LAYOUT	Toni Ihara
PRINTING	Delta Lithograph

Roth, Andrew, 1958-
    Devil's advocates.

    Includes index.
    1. Lawyers--Humor. 2. Lawyers--History.
I. Roth, Jonathan, 1955-   II. Title.
K183.R67 1989 340'.0207
ISBN 0-87337-101-1

89-8764

DEDICATION

To the lawyers who fight for justice and fairness.
We know you are out there somewhere.

ABOUT THE AUTHORS

Andrew Roth is a writer currently working on an anecdotal history of crime in Manhattan. He is a graduate of Occidental College in Los Angeles. Jonathan Roth is a graduate student, writing a doctoral dissertation in Roman History at Columbia University. Both were born and raised in northern California and now live in New York City.

ACKNOWLEDGMENTS

We wish to acknowledge and thank those who have been of help in compiling this book, both for providing us with material and giving us moral support: our publisher Jake Warner, editor Barbara Kate Repa, Mary Randolph and everyone at Nolo Press, our parents Irvin and Maureen Roth and our brother David Roth, Jean-Jacques Aubert, Whitney Bagnall, Alan Cameron, Janet Dunson, William V. Harris, Kathleen Marvin, William McLoughlin, Glenn Nishimura (and everyone at HALT), Lisa Ramaci, Chris Vettel, Steven Vincent and the librarians of the New York Public, Columbia University and Columbia University Law Libraries.

"The startling thing is that lawyers don't seem to like to laugh at themselves, or even get mildly amused about their profession."

—Ann Sleeper, formerly an editor at Little, Brown and Company on rejecting the authors' first book, *Poetic Justice*

INTRODUCTION

Lawyers are upset. They have discovered what they believe to be an alarming new trend: People don't like them. The American Bar Association recently appointed a special panel to investigate the legal profession's bad image. The California State Bar has commissioned a survey to find out why so many people dislike lawyers. Legal conventions now regularly include sessions on the public's negative perception of lawyers.

We wish to reassure lawyers. This wave of anti-lawyer feeling is nothing new. People have always hated you.

Devil's Advocates uncovers the 3,000 year-old tradition of lawyer-hating. It gathers history's best anecdotes, satires, poems and sayings directed against the lawyer. It presents the wit and humor—and honest outrage—of great writers, famous figures and the common people when faced with legal venality.

There have been other histories of the lawyer, but almost all share a common trait: They were written by members of the legal profession—and glowingly slanted in their own favor. Surely some corrective in the depiction of the attorney is needed. *Devil's Advocates* provides material to balance the historical scales.

Of course, there are lawyers who work conscientiously, under difficult conditions, toward a fair and just legal system. There are lawyers, underpaid and unappreciated, who fight for the rights of the poor and oppressed. Unfortunately, they are the rare exception that proves the overwhelming rule. This book assures them just how exceptional they are.

Devil's Advocates serves as a gentle warning to those tempted to solve a problem by going to law, and provides moral support and amusement to those already ensnared in the web of a lawyer. For those who have a lawyer among family or friends, the book offers solace. And if reading this book turns even one young mind from the path of law school toward a healthy and productive life, our work will have been worthwhile.

At the very least, the reader should find it gratifying that *Devil's Advocates* costs only as much as 4 minutes and 37 seconds of a lawyer's time.

TABLE OF CONTENTS

CHAPTER ONE

THE
ANCIENT WORLD

HISTORICAL BRIEFS

A Happy Time Before Lawyers Were Invented

The great civilizations that sprang up in ancient times—in Mesopotamia, Egypt, India, China and elsewhere—all had law courts and plenty of laws. But in those happy times, there was not a single lawyer to be found on the globe. Those involved in lawsuits or accused of crimes represented themselves. The plaintiff stood and stated a case, and the defendant gave a reply. The judge, who might be a priest, a governor, or sometimes even the King, would ask questions of each side to discover the truth—a concept difficult for the modern lawyer to grasp. In ancient times, a verdict was not made strictly in accordance with the technicalities of the law codes, which were intended only for guidance, but according to what the judge considered right, fair and just.

Although there were no lawyers, the wisdom literature of these ancient cultures recognized the traps and travails of the law. These included abuses by corrupt or cruel judges. That judicial corruption existed early on—as if this needed to be proven—is shown by this early hymn to the Babylonian god of justice, Shamash:

> *You give the unscrupulous judge experience of fetters,*
> *Him who accepts a present and yet lets justice miscarry*
> *you make bear his punishment.*[1]

The sages consistently recommended that people settle their disputes amicably, a piece of ancient wisdom which has, unfortunately, been just as consistently ignored to the present day.

AN EPIGRAM FROM EGYPT

The *Instruction of Amen-em-opet* (10th to 7th Century BC) was a popular collection of Egyptian precepts. They were so popular, in fact, that some were plagiarized by the author of the Book of Proverbs in the Bible. The following admonition, from Chapter 20, warns against using lawyerly tactics—even before the invention of the real thing:

> *Do not confuse a man in the law court,*
> *or divert the righteous man.*[2]

PROVERBIAL WISDOM

The following proverb was ascribed to Solomon by the scribe of King Hezekiah (715-687 BC), who copied it:

*What your eyes have seen do not hastily bring into
court: for what will you do in the end, when your
neighbor puts you to shame?
Argue your case with your neighbor himself,
and do not disclose another's secret; lest he who hears
you bring shame upon you, and your ill repute have no
end.*[3]

THE NATURAL NATURE OF THE LAW

A Scythian View

The Scythians were an Iranian people living in what is to-day known as the Caucasus. One of their sages, Anacharsis, who lived around 600 BC, warned:

*Laws are just like spider's webs, they will hold the weak
and delicate who might be caught in their meshes, but
will be torn to pieces by the rich and powerful.*[4]

A Taoist View

Around the same time, but on the other side of the Asian continent, the Chinese philosopher Lao-tze in the Sixth Century BC wrote in his immortal *Tao Te Ching:*

*The more mandates and laws which are enacted,
The more there will be thieves and robbers.*[5]

His fellow philosopher, Confucius (551-479 BC), agreed:

*I can try a lawsuit as well as other men, but surely the
great thing is to bring about that there will be no going
to law.*[6]

ANCIENT GREECE:
THE BIRTHPLACE OF LITIGIOUSNESS

The litigiousness of the Athenians was proverbial even among the ancient Greeks, who were well known in the ancient world for their habit of suing each other at the drop of a Phrygian cap. In many of his comic plays, Aristophanes made fun of the Attic preoccupation with litigation. For example, in his play *The Peace,* the character Trygaeus said: "You Athenians do nothing but try cases." And when, in *The Clouds,* Socrates pointed out Athens to Strepsiades on a map, which was something of a novelty at that time, Strepsiades said: "I don't believe it for I see no juries sitting." More early disdain spouted from Euelpides, who, in *The Birds,* observed: "Grasshoppers chirp upon their boughs a month or two, but our Athenians chirp over their lawsuits their whole life long."[7]

Not surprisingly, then, it was in Greece that the first unfortunate steps down the path that led to the invention of lawyers were taken. As a side effect of the growing popularity of philosophical schools, people began to study rhetoric, and some of these "rhetors"—a sort of proto-lawyer—began to write speeches for those involved in trials, although the plaintiff or defendant still had to read them in court. Demosthenes, Lysias and Isocrates were a few of these early, behind-the-scenes legal engineers. In a very short time, the rhetors saw themselves as professional legal experts, very close to the modern concept of lawyer and often identical in spirit. Modern translations often refer to them as "lawyers."

A SOCRATIC MONOLOGUE

Socrates (469-399 BC), the father of western philosophy, was wise enough to dislike lawyers, although he was not above using many of their disputatious techniques:

> *[Lawyers are] always in a hurry—for the water flowing through the water-clock urges them on—and the other party in the suit does not permit them to talk about anything they please, but stands over them exercising the law's compulsion by reading the brief from which no deviation is allowed . . . and their discourse is always about a fellow slave and is addressed to a master who sits there holding some case or other in his hands; and the contests never run an indefinite course, but are always directed at some point at issue, and often the race is for the defendant's life. As a result of all this, the speakers become tense and shrewd; they know how to wheedle their masters with words and gain his favor by acts; but in their souls they become small and warped. For they have been deprived of growth and straightforwardness and independence by the slavery they have endured from their youths up, for this forces them to do crooked acts by putting a great burden of fears and dangers upon their souls while these are still tender; and since they cannot bear this burden with uprightness and truth, they turn forthwith to deceit and to requiting wrong with wrong, so that they become greatly bent and stunted. Consequently, they pass from youth to manhood with no soundness of mind in them, but they think they have become clever and wise.[8]*

SELECTIONS FROM A MASTER

Aristophanes (c. 450-385 BC)

As mentioned above, Aristophanes, the comic playwright of classical Athens, described the new proto-lawyers in suitably unflattering terms in many of his plays. In *The Clouds,* for example, which was staged in 423 BC, the character Strepsiades is addressing Socrates. He wants to learn rhetoric to escape his debts. If he does, then he'll become:

Bold, hasty and wise, a concocter of lies,
A rattler to speak, a dodger, a sneak,
A regular claw of the tables of law,
A shuffler complete, well worn in deceit,
A supple, unprincipled, troublesome cheat;
A hang-dog accurst, a bore with the worst,
In the tricks of the jury-court thoroughly versed.

Then the Chorus gets to the point:

Yes, and men shall come and wait
In their thousands at your gate,
Desiring consultations and advice
On an action or a pleading,
From the men of light and leading
And you'll pocket many talents in a trice.[9]

MEDICAL METAPHOR

Not all the Greeks took legal argumentation with such good humor. Euripides, the tragic playwright (c. 485-406 BC), argued that the mere presence of an advocate showed that the client was trying to hide something:

A just cause needs no interpreting. It carries its own case. But the unjust argument, since it is sick, needs clever medicine.[10]

THE PLATONIC RELATIONSHIP WITH LAWYERS

Plato (c. 427-347 BC), the second great name in Greek philosophy, recorded and interpreted the views of his teacher Socrates. In one selection from *The Republic,* Socrates and Glaucon discuss the wastefulness of litigation. It is unfortunate that although many people, including lawyers and litigants-to-be, have read Plato, no one seems to follow his advice:

Socrates: Could anything show a more shameful lack of culture than to have so little justice in oneself that one must get it from others, who thus become masters and judges over one?

Glaucon: There could be no worse disgrace.

Socrates: Or is there a lower depth, when, not content with spending most of his life in courts of law as plaintiffs or defendants, a man is actually led to take a vulgar pride in being so litigious; one who fancies himself as an expert in dishonesty, up to every turn and twist that will enable him to evade punishment, and all for the sake of trivial or worthless ends, because he does not know how much better it is so to order men's life, as never to stand in need of a drowsy judge.[11]

"The good have no need of an advocate."

Phocian (c. 402-317 BC), Athenian statesman[12]

DOUBLE DEALING

Early on, lawyers displayed a disturbing willingness to argue either—or both—sides of a dispute, as noted by historian William Forsyth:

It is a common charge to bring against advocates at the present day, that they will indifferently espouse and argue upon either side of a question; but what shall we say of the speech-writers at Athens, who sometimes composed orations for both the contending parties in the same cause?

We possess three sets of tetralogies, or quartettes of speeches, which Antiphon wrote for the prosecution and defense in cases of trials for homicide; and an old scholiast mentions this approvingly, as a great feat of dexterity and skill. He says: "It is true that Antiphon always exhibits his native and peculiar power, but especially in those speeches, in which he counterpleads against himself. For having prepared two speeches on behalf of the accuser, he composed two for the accused also, and sustained his high reputation in both alike.[13]

No doubt he billed twice.

NEITHER A BURROWER NOR A BARRISTER BE

Lawyers, at least in the sense of burrowers into the law, were not a curse confined to the West in ancient times. The great historian of the Han Dynasty of China, Ssu-ma Chien (145-c. 90 BC), in his *Shih-Chih (Record of the Historian)*, tells the story of Chang Tang, who ended up as the Chief Justice of the

Chinese Empire. Like many lawyers, he showed early promise in his calling:

> *Chang Tang of Tu was the son of the assistant magistrate of Changan. One day when he was a child his father left him to mind the house, only to find on his return that a rat had stolen a piece of meat. In anger he beat his son. Then Chang Tang dug out the rat hole, found the guilty rat and what remained of the meat, tried the rat, recorded its confession and decided on its punishment. He then took the rat and meat into the yard, where he passed sentence and executed the culprit. His father, observing this, was amazed to find that the records read like those drawn up by an experienced scrivener. So he set the lad to writing legal documents . . . .*[14]

Ssu-ma Chien also describes some proto-shysters of the Celestial Kingdom:

> *Whenever Chi An [another government official] argued with Chang Tang, the Chief Justice split hairs about the law, whereas Chi An kept stubbornly to principles and refused to compromise. He would fume: "How right people are to say that pen-pushers should never be made high officials! If Chang Tang had his way, no one would dare take a step forward or look men straight in the eye." . . . He [Chi An] declared that those pettifoggers twisted the law to ruin men, obscuring the truth to win credit for themselves at the expense of the people.*[15]

"One lawsuit begets another."

Latin Proverb[16]

LAWYERS ARE INVENTED: ROME BEGINS TO FALL

During the rise of Rome, its citizens involved in lawsuits pleaded their own cases, as was true everywhere in the ancient world. But like the Greeks, the Romans could call on legal experts to assist in a case. These experts were called *advocati*—literally, "men called to one's side." According to the *lex cincia* passed by the Senate in 204 BC, the *advocati* were forbidden from taking fees. But in the Second Century BC, a fateful step was taken: In some cases, an *advocatus* could speak on another's behalf in court in exchange for a fee. This was the birth of the the paid mouthpiece, the tongue for hire, the juridical mercenary, the lawyer *qua* lawyer.

The *lex cincia* became more and more a dead letter and by 100 BC, the Roman advocates were professionally speaking for others so regularly that they came to be called *causidici*, or "speakers of cases." Recognizing the danger that a professional

class of lawyers posed to the Roman Empire, Caesar Augustus (63 BC-14 AD), revived the *lex cincia,* but soon lawyers were again ignoring the law. Another attempt to abolish legal fees was initiated in 47 AD. During a Senate debate of the issue, Senator Gaius Silius said:

> *If no one paid a fee for lawsuits, there would be less of them! As it is, feuds, charges, malevolence and slander are encouraged. For just as physical illness brings revenue to doctors, so a diseased legal system entices advocates.*[17]

Although the Senate passed the law, the Emperor Claudius (10 BC to 54 AD), popularly dubbed "The Lawyers' Emperor," vetoed the legislation.

And we are still suffering the consequences.

THE ROGUES GALLERY

Quintus Hortensius Hortalus (114-50 BC)

"The highest law is often the greatest roguery."

Publius Terentius Afer (c. 190-159 BC), Roman playwright[18]

Hortensius was the most prominent lawyer in Rome, rising to the head of the bar—and indeed to the consulship, the highest office in Rome—by dint of his oratorical skills and a complete lack of morals. He considered bribery a perfectly legitimate means of winning suits. The fact that in late Republican Rome this was not considered unusual shows merely, as Alphonse Karr observed, that "the more things change, the more they stay the same."

The Romans gained their great empire by means of military prowess; those who rose to high office did so by winning great wars and conquering territories. But Hortensius, like lawyers throughout the ages, felt that discretion was the better part of valor. While victories won in court were perhaps not as glorious as those on the battlefield, they were certainly as profitable, considerably less dangerous and saved wear and tear on the toga.

By the 70s BC, Hortensius had become the leading orator in Rome, using the florid and theatrical "Asiatic" style, and resorting to shameless bribery of juries and judges. As Cicero, who prosecuted Verres, put it:

> *With only a moderate rhetorical training, and with even less natural endowment, yet by hard work and application and especially by careful use of his political influence in ensuring the success of his pleas, he was for some time one of the leaders of the bar.*

One of Hortensius' clients, Terentius Varro, was accused and undoubtedly guilty of extortion. Hortensius obtained an acquittal by bribing the jury. He also convicted innocent defendants through bribery, and one of his victims, the high-born Quintus Calidius, complained ironically: "It is not possible to decently convict a man of praetorian rank for less than 30,000 silver pieces."[19]

The high (or low) point in his career was his defense, along with Lucullus and Sisenna, of Gaius Verres, the cruel and corrupt governor of Sicily. Verres, flagrant in his disregard of the law, once remarked: "What I steal the first year goes to increase my own fortune, but the profits of the second year go to lawyers and defense counsels, and the whole of the third year's take, the largest, is reserved for the judges."[20]

Verres was indicted, technically, for embezzling 1,000,000 silver pieces—although the evidence showed this was obviously a conservative estimate. According to Cicero, however, embezzlement was only one of Verres' crimes. Among his other ignoble acts were crucifying Roman citizens, tax fraud, receiving protection money from pirates and systematic looting. In addition, Verres, who fancied himself an art connoisseur, vigorously "collected" most of the island's valuable artwork.

Hortensius' client was embarrassingly guilty. The defense was not overly worried, though, because buying acquittals from the Senatorial juries had become standard operating procedure. Unfortunately for him, Senatorial corruption had become a political issue, and there was a bill in the Senate to turn the extortion trials over to the Equestrian Order of the Roman Knights. So Verres and his well-paid lawyers were faced, to their horror, with a jury that refused to be bribed.

In the true slippery style of the defense attorney, Hortensius tried trick after trick, both windward and leeward of the law, to get his client off. He tried to have one of Verres' lackeys, a man named Caelius, appointed as prosecutor in the case. But Cicero, well-known for his eloquence, convinced the Senate to appoint him as prosecutor. Hortensius then unsuccessfully tried to bribe Cicero. Since Hortensius had been elected consul for the next year (amid charges of vote-buying) and this office would allow him to appoint the judge for the case, he tried to postpone the trial into his consulship by bringing an embezzlement case against the ex-governor of Greece, hoping to slap together a case before Cicero was ready. As only one case of this type could be tried at a time, Verres' case would be delayed until the next year. But Cicero had his brief ready too quickly, and Hortensius was again thwarted.

Hortensius then tried to delay the actual trial by dragging out the defense. But again, Cicero was not to be outmaneu-

HORTENSIVS

vered, and the trial lasted only a week or so before Hortensius threw in the towel. Cicero is generally said to have won this case, although, in fact, Verres was not convicted, and went into voluntary exile with most of his loot to Marseilles. There he lived comfortably for almost thirty years.

After the Verres case, Hortensius actually joined Cicero in defending many political cases—including those of Rabirius, accused of high treason; Publius Cornelius Sulla, accused of conspiracy to overthrow the state; and Publius Sestius, accused of political strong-arming and bribery. All were acquitted, and the fact that blatant crimes against the state went unpunished did a lot to bring an end to the Roman Republic.

Hortensius died in 50 BC, just before the outbreak of the civil war that brought Julius Caesar to power. His timing was good. Verres, his former client, was executed by order of Marc Antony in 43 BC, allegedly because Antony coveted some of his *objets d'art*—no doubt part of the Sicilian loot.[21]

TRICKS OF A SORDID TRADE

Even as the legal cabal was being born, tried and true strategems for freeing the guilty, blaming the innocent and obscuring the facts were already being put to profitable use. Perhaps the earliest "insiders' guide" to such techniques is the handbook for lawyers titled *To Herennius,* written between 86 and 82 BC. The work was first erroneously attributed to Cicero; its unknown author is now commonly referred to as "Pseudo-Cicero."

> *Now I must explain the Subtle Approach. There are three occasions on which we cannot use the Direct Opening, and these we must consider carefully: 1) when our cause is discreditable, that is, when the subject itself alienates the hearer from us; 2) when the hearer has apparently been won over by the previous speakers of the opposition; 3) or when the hearer has become wearied by listening to the previous speakers.*

> *If the cause has a discreditable character, we can make our introduction with the following points: that the agent, not the action, ought to be considered . . . .*

> *The defendant's counsel will first show his client's upright life if he can; if he cannot, he will have recourse to thoughtlessness, folly, youth, force or undue influence. On these matters . . . censure ought not to be imposed for conduct extraneous to the present charge. If the speaker is seriously handicapped by the man's baseness and notoriety, he will first take care to say that false*

rumors have been spread about an innocent man, and will use the commonplace that rumors ought not to be believed. If none of these pleas are practicable, let him say that he is not discussing the man's morals before censors, but the charges of his opponents before jurors.[22]

LAWYERS WHO KNOW NO LAW

Cicero (106-43 BC), is probably the most famous, and arguably one of the best, of the Roman lawyers. In his essay *On Oratory*, published in 55 BC, he complained about lawyers who don't know their law—a situation that endures to the present day:

> *As for the rest [of the lawyers] I shall not hesitate to give my vote for a verdict of guilty first of laziness, and secondly of effrontery as well. For to flit around the courts, to loiter about the Bench and tribunals of the judges, to engage in civil proceedings involving weighty interests in which the dispute is often not as to facts but as to equity and law, to vaunt oneself in cases before the Civil Court where are debated the rights concerning fair use, guardianship, clanship, relationship through males, alluvial accessions, the formation of islands, obligations, sales, party-walls, ancient lights, rain-drip from the eaves, the revocation or establishment of wills, and all those other matters innumerable, when a man is wholly ignorant as to what is his own and what another's and even of the essential difference between the citizen and foreigner, this is the mark of no ordinary effrontery . . . .*
>
> *Accordingly, that a man, ignorant of these and similar laws of his own community, should roam with a large following from court to court, haughtily and with head upraised, eager and assured in mien and countenance, directing his gaze hither and thither, and holding out and tendering protection to clients, aid to friends and illumination of his talent and advice to wellnigh every citizen, is not all this to be considered something supremely scandalous?*[23]

"When you have no basis for an argument, abuse the plaintiff."

Cicero[24]

THE PUMPKINIFICATION OF THE DIVINE CLAUDIUS

Lucius Annaeus Seneca (8 BC-65 AD), born at Corduba in Spain, is known mainly for his philosophical writings and tragic dramas, neither of which are particularly sympathetic to the legal profession. He wrote, for example: "The lawyer prays for dissensions and makes up his fortune through corruption."[25] His most extended attack on lawyers is in a satirical piece on the death of the emperor Claudius, who was known as, and often derided as, an amateur legal scholar. Claudius delighted in personally judging cases. This selection is from the work the *Apocolocyntosis* or *Pumpkinification of the Divine Claudius*. In it, the god Mercury leads the deceased Claudius down into the underworld. On the way, they meet the funeral procession for Claudius:

> *It was certainly an extraordinary spectacle, done at great cost, so that you could plainly see that a god was being buried: there was such great crowds of trumpeters, horn-blowers and players of all sorts of brass instruments, all playing at the same time, that even Claudius could hear it. Everyone was joyful and happy—the Roman people walked around like free men. Only Agatho and a few lawyers were crying, but their grief was plainly heartfelt. The legal experts were coming out of the shadows, pale and thin, being barely alive, looking like people just brought back to life. And one of them, when he saw the lawyers putting their heads together and lamenting their misfortune, walked up and said: "Didn't I tell you that the party wouldn't last forever?"*

The lawyers sing a dirge for Claudius:

> *Mourn for the man! None other*
> *Could decide cases faster,*
> *Even hearing only one side,*
> *Or neither. Who now, as judge,*
> *Will hear lawsuits all year long?*
> *Now the one who ruled a hundred Cretan towns,*
> *and judges the silent dead, must yield his seat to you.*
> *Beat your breasts with gloomy palms*
> *O you lawyers, the venal tribe.*[26]

HE SAID IT

The Palestine in which Jesus of Nazareth (c. 6 BC–c. 30 AD), lived was part of the Roman Empire and subject to its laws. The lawyers he berates in the New Testament are not Roman lawyers, but rather the experts on Jewish law who "strain after a gnat and swallow a camel." It is noteworthy that someone who suffered tax collectors and sinners to come unto him drew the line at lawyers:

One of the lawyers answered him, "Teacher in saying
this you reproach us also." And he said, "Woe to you
lawyers also! for you load men with burdens hard to
bear, and you yourselves do not touch the burdens with
one of your fingers . . . . Woe to you lawyers! for you
have taken away the key of knowledge; you did not
enter yourselves, and you hindered those who were
entering."[27]

SPARE THE ROD, LOSE THE CASE

The practice of hauling weeping wives and children into
court for sympathy has a very long history, and was common in
Roman courts. Quintilian (Marcus Fabius Quintilianus, 42-118)
mentions such an attempt at pathos by Glycon Spiridion that
had only bathetic results. In the midst of an impassioned appeal,
he had a boy brought into court in tears, as though weeping for
the loss of the parents who Glycon lionized. Asked why he cried
so piteously, the child, being badly trained in his part, answered:
"Because my tutor is pinching me."[28]

IT'S BETTER TO MEDIATE THAN TO BURN

In his first letter to the Corinthians, St. Paul rebukes his
fellow Christians who, in spite of the presence of the Holy Spirit,
insist on suing each other:

When one of you has a grievance against a brother,
does he dare go to law before the unrighteous instead of
the saints? Do you not know that the saints will judge
the world? And if the world is to be judged by you, are
you incompetent to try trivial cases? Do you not know
that we are to judge angels? How much more, matters
pertaining to this life! If, then, you have such cases, why
do you lay them before those who are least esteemed by
the church? I say this to your shame. Can it be that there
is no man among you wise enough to decide between
members of the brotherhood, but brother goes to law
against brother, and that before unbelievers? To have
lawsuits at all with one another is defeat for you. Why
not rather suffer wrong? Why not rather be defrauded?
But you yourself wrong and defraud and that even your
own brother.[29]

THE LABYRINTH OF LEGAL LANGUAGE

The Sound and the Fury

This is probably the most famous ancient comment on lawyers, cribbed by Marcus Valerius Martial (c. 40-104) from a Greek epigram of the age of Nero. In it, Martial complains that his lawyer's overblown rhetoric is missing the point:

Not for assault, or murder, or poisoning,
Rather my lawsuit is about three goats.
I claim they were stolen by my thieving neighbor.
This fact the judge wishes proven to him:
You, in a great voice and with both hands,
Sound off about Cannae and the Mithridatic war,
And the perjuries of Punic frenzy,
And about Sullas and Mariuses and Muciuses.
Now, Postumus, talk about my three goats.[30]

THE DELAY OF THE LAW

The Length of Latin Litigation

A problem in ancient, as in modern times: It is far easier to get into a lawsuit than out of one. This is from Martial's seventh book of epigrams:

A lawsuit grinds you, Gargilianus, numbering
twenty cold winters, one suit in three courts,
Wretched and demented man! Litigating for twenty years,
Gargilianus, could anyone give in?[31]

RAGS AND RICHES OF THE ROMAN BAR

Decimus Junius Juvenalis (c. 50-c. 130), who wrote satires on Roman daily life, mocked the poor, starving *causidici* scraping a meager living, often taking their fees in kind and scrambling for cases—chariot-chasing, as it were:

Tell me, then, what does pleading in court and carrying briefs in huge bundles get for the lawyer? Those fellows talk big, especially when someone they owe money is listening, or if a potential litigant, coming along with a big ledger to collect a dubious debt, taps them on the shoulder. Then their puffed cheeks bellow with exaggerated boasts . . . . But if you want to figure out their real worth, then compare the fortunes of a hundred lawyers with that of one successful charioteer.

While the great men sit around, you stand up, like a second-rate Ajax, and plead a case of disputed manumission before a bumpkin judge. Go ahead, burst your lungs, you poor fool. So that, worn out by your labor, you can chalk up another little victory. And what is the fee for your pleading? The price of a little dried-up ham, or a jar of tuna-fish? Or a month's worth of old onions, or five bottles of cheap wine? And when you've managed four cases, and maybe earned a gold piece, then a big slice goes, according to your contract, to the solicitors . . . .

Other Roman lawyers, dressed in the finest of togas, represented the richest and most powerful senators (and were generally senators themselves), surrounded by secretaries and assistants, and demanded the highest fees allowed under the *lex cincia*, which regulated them. As Juvenal points out, their higher fees were not necessarily based on higher ability:

The noble Aemilius will demand the maximum fee, though even I'm a better lawyer than he. But then he has a bronze four-horse chariot in his courtyard . . . . In the end such things are useful: purple or violet robes bring in business for the lawyer. It is generally agreed that it pays to live ostentatiously beyond one's means . . . . Shouldn't we put our trust in talent? Nowadays, no one would give Cicero himself two hundred coppers unless he had a big shiny ring on his finger. The first thing a potential client looks for is: have you got eight slaves, or ten assistants? Do you have a sedan-chair, with men in togas clearing the way? . . . It's rare to find a smooth talker in a thin cloak.[33]

THE LAWYER AS ADJECTIVE

When criticizing his own writing to his teacher, the Emperor Marcus Aurelius Antoninus (121-180), wrote tellingly:

I wrote a wretched little piece, which I ought to dedicate to the water-nymphs or to Vulcan: truly today I have

"No commodity was so publicly for sale as the perfidy of lawyers."

Gaius Cornelius Tacitus (c. 55-c. 117) Roman historian[32]

been unlucky in my writing, the scribblings of a hunter
or a grape picker . . . absolutely lawyer-like in odium
and tedium.[34]

THE LABYRINTH OF
LEGAL LANGUAGE

Gaius was one of the most renowned Roman jurists, although nothing is known of him except his first name and that he lived in the Second Century AD. He wrote a textbook for law students called the *Institutes,* and in it discussed the ridiculous verbal inflexibility of Roman law:

> *It was decided that a man who, having brought a suit*
> *regarding vines which had been cut down, used the*
> *word "vines" in his pleas, should have his case*
> *dismissed, because he ought to have used the word*
> *"trees"' in it, because the law of the Twelve Tables,*
> *according to which the action regarding cut-down vines*
> *was sought, speaks of "cut down trees . . . ."*[35]

THE LAW FIDDLES WHILE ROME BURNS

Some historians theorize that corruption or lead poisoning led to the fall of the Roman Empire. Others have suggested that after four hundred years of Roman law, the inhabitants welcomed the barbarians. The following anecdote bears out the theory of the welcome barbarians. Priscus of Panium was a high official of the Eastern Roman Empire in the Fifth Century. He wrote a book, *Byzantine History,* which described, among other things, the empire's final years:

> *When Priscus of Panium visited Attila's camp as*
> *ambassador in 448, he was surprised to be greeted in*
> *Greek by a man dressed as a Hun. It turned out that he*
> *was a Greek who had settled at Viminacum on the*
> *Danube and prospered as a merchant. When the city*
> *was sacked by the Huns he had been taken prisoner; his*
> *Hunnish master had later set him free, and he had*
> *decided not to return to the empire but to live among the*
> *Huns. When Priscus reproached him as a renegade, he*
> *justified his conduct on two grounds, the exorbitant*
> *taxation which Roman citizens had to pay, and the*
> *abuses of the Roman courts of justice. "The laws are not*
> *the same for all," he declared. "If a rich man breaks the*
> *law he can avoid paying the penalty for his wrong-*
> *doing. But if it is a poor man, who does not know how*
> *to pull strings, he suffers the penalty of the law—unless*

*he departs this life before the trial, while proceedings
drag on interminably and vast expenses are incurred.
That is the most monstrous thing of all, to have to pay
for justice. An injured party cannot get a hearing unless
he pays money to the judge and to his officials.* '[36]

NOTES

1 W.G. Lambert, *Babylonian Wisdom Literature*, Oxford University Press, London, 1960, pg. 133. Translated by W.G. Lambert.

2 James B. Pritchard, *The Ancient Near East, An Anthology of Texts and Pictures*, Vol. 1, Princeton University Press, Princeton, 1958, pg. 242. Translated by John A. Wilson.

3 Proverbs *25:8*, Revised Standard Version.

4 Plutarch, *Life of Solon* 5.2, in *Plutarch's Lives*, Vol. I, Loeb Classical Library, Harvard University Press, Cambridge, 1982, pg. 415. Translated by Bernadette Perrin.

5 Lao-Tze, *Tao Te Ching*, Chapter 57, quoted in Laurence J. Peter, *Peter's Quotations*, Bantam Books, New York, 1979, pg. 292.

6 Confucius, *Analects* XII.13, in *The Analects of Confucius*, Paragon Book Reprint, New York, 1968 (originally published Shansi, China,1910), pg. 585. Translated by William E. Soothill.

7 Aristophanes, *The Peace*, l.504; *The Clouds*, ll.207-8; *The Birds*, ll. 39-42, from *Aristophanes*, Vols. I and II, Loeb Classical Library, Harvard University Press, Cambridge,1978, Translated by Benjamin Bickley Rogers.

8 Plato, *Thaeatetus* 172E, from *Plato*, Vol. VII, Loeb Classical Library, Harvard University Press, Cambridge, 1977, pgs. 117-18. Translated by Harold N. Fowler.

9 Aristophanes, *Clouds*, ll. 445-450, 467-475, Loeb Classical Library, Harvard University Press, Cambridge, 1978. Translated by Benjamin Bickley Rogers.

10 Euripides, *Phoenician Women*, ll. 469-472, from Rhoda T. Tripp (ed.), *The International Thesaurus of Quotations*, Thomas Y. Crowell, New York, 1970, pg. 345. Translated by Elizabeth Wykoff.

11 Plato, Republic III.405, in *The Republic of Plato*, Oxford University Press, London, 1973, pg. 95. Translated by Francis N. Cornford.

12 Plutarch, *Apothegms*, "Sayings of Phocian" Section 10, from *Bartlett's Quotations*, Emily M. Beck (ed.), Little, Brown and Co., Boston,1968, pg. 96.

13 William Forsyth, *The History of Lawyers: Ancient and Modern*, James Cockcroft & Co., New York, 1875, pg. 50.

14 Ssu-ma Chien, *Records of the Historian*, Foreign Language Press, Peking, 1979. pgs. 442-44. Translated by Yang-Hsien-Yi and Gladys Yang.

15 Ssu-ma Chien, *Records of the Historian*, pg. 350. Translated by Yang Hsien-Yi and Gladys Yang.

16 W. Gurney Benham, *Benham's Book of Quotations*, Cassell & Co., New York, 1907, pg. 613a.

17 Tacitus, *The Annals of Imperial Rome*, Penguin Books, Harmondsworth, 1956, pg. 233. Translated by Michael Grant.

18 *Benham's Book of Quotations*, pg. 573.

19 Cicero, *Against Verres* I.12.38, Loeb Classical Library, Harvard University Press, Cambridge, 1978, pg. 105. Translated by L.H.G. Greenwood.

20 Cicero, *Against Verres* I.14.40, pg. 107.

21 Cicero, Brutus, Loeb Classical Library, Harvard University Press, Cambridge, 1961, pgs. 261 ff. Translated by G.L. Hendrickson. and Dr. F. Von Der Meuhl, "Hortensius," *Paulys Real-Encyclopaedie*, Wilhelm Kroll (ed.), Stuttgardt, 1913, Vol. 8, pgs. 2470-81.

22 Pseudo-Cicero, *Rhetorica Ad Herennium*, I.1.6; II.3.5, Loeb Classical Library, Harvard University Press, Cambridge, 1977. Translated by Harry Caplan.

23 Cicero, De Oratore, I.38.173-3, I.55.236, Loeb Classical Library, Harvard University Press, 1976. pgs. 119, 169-70. Translated by E.W. Sutton.

24 Cicero, *Pro Flacco* 10, from Seldes, *The Great Quotations*, pg. 158.

25 Edward P. Day, *Day's Collacon: An Encyclopedia of Prose Quotations*, International, New York, 1884, pg. 496.

26 Seneca, *Apocolocyntosis 12.* Translated by J. Roth.

27 Luke 11:46, Revised Standard Version.

28 Quintilian, Institutio Oratia IV.1.41, from *Quintilian*, Vol. II, Loeb Classical Library, Harvard University Press, 1971, pg. 409. Translated by H.E. Butler.

29 St. Paul, First Letter to the Corinthians 6.1-7, Revised Standard Version.

30 Martial, *Epigrams*, VI.19. Translated by J. Roth.

31 Martial, *Epigrams*, VII.65. Translated by J. Roth.

32 Tacitus, *Annals*, XI.5. Translated by J. Roth.

33 Juvenal, *Satires* VII.105-49. Translated by J. Roth.

34 Cornelius Fronto, *To Marcus Caesar* IV.5. Translated by J. Roth.

35 Gaius, *Institutes*, IV.11. Translated by J. Roth and J.J. Aubert.

36 Priscus, *Byzantine History*, VIII.86-88. From A.H.M. Jones,
    Later Roman Empire, Johns Hopkins University Press,
    Baltimore, 1986, pg. 516.

CHAPTER TWO

THE
MIDDLE AGES

HISTORICAL BRIEF

Friendly Representation

Anglo-Saxon law was based on trial by ordeal, in which the accused were exposed to physical dangers supposed to be harmless to the innocent. Not surprisingly, there were few lawyers to be found when questions of guilt or innocence depended upon being thrown into a lake, plunging a hand into boiling water, or carrying a red-hot iron bar in the palm. But these early Germanic legal procedures came in two parts: Before the actual ordeal, there was a proceeding to hear the two sides, decide if there was need for a trial and pinpoint the actual issues involved. Defendants or plaintiffs could bring along friends to verify their oaths. This was not to corroborate any testimony, but only to pledge that the oath-taker was sincere. Eventually, it seems, these people began not only to attest to an oath, but to speak in favor of their friends. From here it was just a short step to the ancestor of the modern attorney, the professional "friend" for hire.

HURRY UP AND DIE

Meanwhile, on the Continent, Roman law and the *causidici* and *advocati* that lurked within it survived the fall of the Roman Empire. Standing above these courts, however, there were now "barbarian" kings who did not often hesitate to intervene to oil the slow, grinding wheels of the law. An anecdote was told by John Malalas (491-578), a Byzantine historian from Syria. It took place in the days of King Theodoric (c. 454-526), who founded the Ostrogothic Kingdom in Italy in 493.

> *Juvenalia was a woman of senatorial rank, who for thirty long years had been involved in a lawsuit with a patrician named Firmus. Finally Juvenalia petitioned the king for a speedy settlement of the case. Theodoric summoned the lawyers for each side and gave them two days to settle the case, under penalty of death. Thus motivated, the lawyers worked out a judgment within the time limit. Afterwards when Juvenalia came to thank the king, he summoned the lawyers. "Why," he asked, "did you not do in thirty years what you have done in two days?" When they were unable to answer, he had them executed.*[1]

AS LONG AS YOU BOTH SHALL LIVE

While the Western Empire broke down into feudal kingdoms and baronies, the Eastern Greek-speaking half continued under the old tradition of Rome, becoming the Byzantine Empire. The plague of the law's delay also ravaged the Byzantine courts. The Emperor, his hands tied by red tape, could not use the same primitive yet effective medicine that Theodoric prescribed. He could only issue proclamations. Emperor Justinian (483-565), made the following one in 530:

> *It seems to us a case ought to be hastened, lest lawsuits become almost immortal and exceed the length of a man's life . . . we order therefore, that no lawsuit concerning money be protracted more than three years past the point when the suit was brought.*[2]

As in most systems essentially controlled by lawyers, so many exceptions were granted that the decree quickly became a dead letter.

THE LABYRINTH OF LEGAL LANGUAGE

During the Early Middle Ages, from around 500 to 800, it was the Irish who led Europe in jurisprudence. The Irish *brehons*, Gaelic for jurist, wrote many legal textbooks and commentaries. Like all lawyers, the *brehons* guarded their monopoly on law most often through an abuse of language. As legal historian René A. Wormser related:

> *Many of their lawbooks were unintelligible to the uninitiated; the words and sentences were scrambled, so that one could not read them without knowing a code. Many of the manuscripts which have been discovered have taken as long as fifty years to decipher.*[3]

ROGUES GALLERY

Eyjolf Bolverksson (c. 970-1012)

All that is known of Eyjolf Bolverksson, once "one of the three greatest lawyers in Iceland," is related in *Njal's Saga*, written by an anonymous Icelandic author in the Thirteenth Century. Although portrayed as handsome, tall and nobly-born, Eyjolf had a character flaw common to his calling: He was "very fond of money."

Iceland, during the Eleventh Century, was an independent republic—all freeholders had a vote in the *Althing* or assembly. The real power, though, was in the hands of the wealthy chieftains, and the sagas are full of stories of their blood feuds and battles. *Njal's Saga* is noteworthy for its detailed description of lawsuits and trials, where the Norse heroes battled it out in court, represented by bold Viking lawyers.

Eyjolf was introduced in the story when a rich chieftain named Flosi Thordarson wanted to be defended in a scandalous multiple murder case. The murders had been the result of a long-standing feud between Flosi and the sons of the hero, Njal. Flosi led an attack on Njal's farm and, unable to defeat the hero and the brave Njalssons, decided to burn the house down with the family inside— a particularly dastardly violation of the Icelandic code of chivalry. Some of the household were let out of the house, but Flosi sneaked up behind the one son who had come out, and chopped off his head. The rest of the family was burned to death.

A friend of the family named Kari Solmundarson escaped the burning building and organized the prosecution of Flosi and the other murderers. He then obtained the services of a famous lawyer named Mord Valgardson to lead the prosecution team. The trial was to be held at the annual *Althing*, and all the kinsmen of both sides streamed to the site. There were not many lawyers in Iceland, and fewer that would defend a scoundrel like Flosi. Recognizing the universal advantage of wealth over truth, however, Flosi sought out Eyjolf at the *Althing*. He had no trouble picking out the lawyer in the crowd, as Eyjolf was wearing the Viking version of a Brooks Brothers suit and designer briefcase: "a scarlet cloak and gold headband, carrying a silver-wrought axe." Flosi began at once flattering the lawyer, referring to his noble heritage, but Eyjolf replied: "You speak handsomely, but I don't propose to have anything to do with any business of yours."

Flosi understood some basic legal psychology, though, and produced a heavy gold bracelet, which he placed on Eyjolf's arm. This changed matters instantly. "Since you behave so generously," the lawyer purred, "it is only reasonable of me to accept the bracelet, and you can also take it for granted that I shall take up the defense in your case and do everything that is required."

Eyjolf had his work cut out for him, as the case against Flosi seemed airtight and public opinion was against the murderer. Njal had been very popular and had done his best to end the feud. Despite Flosi's attempts to win support by spreading money around, his conviction and a harsh sentence seemed certain.

Nevertheless, the lawyer started right in earning his bracelet by thinking up a neat legal trick. At the time, Iceland was divided into four judicial districts, with a Fifth Court for appeals. All the principals lived, and the crime occurred, in the East Quarter, so naturally the prosecution would institute the suit there. Eyjolf advised Flosi to resign his chieftancy, turn it over to his brother and then attach himself to a chieftain in the North Quarter, thus changing his legal residence. This was to be kept secret, as Eyjolf warned:

> *If they don't get to know it, then maybe they will commit a fatal error. . . . They are likely to overlook this point and a Fifth Court charge will be lodged against them if they plead their suit in any court but the correct one. We shall press the charge then, but not before it is absolutely necessary.*

The indictment was then served by the unsuspecting prosecution in the East Quarter Court.

Mord formally instituted proceedings, and a legal battle ensued over the seating of jurors. Under the law, if any of the jurors were sucessfully dismissed, a verdict could not be given and the suit would be invalidated on a technicality. Three challenges were made by Eyjolf, but in each case Mord defended the seating of the jurors. "The general opinion," so the saga goes, "was that Mord had handled the suit very well, but that Flosi and his men were using mainly tricks and technicalities."

The jury brought in a verdict of guilty. But Flosi was not perturbed. He said to Eyjolf: "I must laugh when I think of the wry faces they will make and the way they will scratch their heads when you present the defense." Then Eyjolf pulled the legal rabbit out of his helmet: He brought suit against Mord and the prosecution for filing the case in the wrong court. This sleight-of-hand worked perfectly and the guilty verdict was set aside.

Eyjolf's legal trickery was very successful. Flosi beat the rap on the murder charge. But as in modern Mafia trials, the prosecution, having failed to make the homicide indictment stick, decided to try the culprit on a lesser charge. The prosecution heard about the golden arm bracelet, despite Eyjolf's attempts to keep it secret. Like modern English barristers, Icelandic lawyers were not allowed to take direct payment for their services, so the prosecution brought a suit against Flosi for bribing Eyjolf to take his defense.

This trial was held in the Fifth Court. Conviction on the bribery charge looked certain, but Eyjolf decided on one more legal trick. There were forty-eight judges in this court, but each side was supposed to exclude six, leaving thirty-six. The defense refused to exclude any judges, in which case the prosecution was required to dismiss six for the defense. Eyjolf counted on Mord, in his haste for a conviction, overlooking this technicality. This in fact occurred, and Eyjolf triumphantly moved to have the suit thrown out of court.

Since the murderers managed to get completely off the hook through legal maneuvering, one of the members of the prosecution team opted for a more direct approach to justice. Seizing a spear, he killed one of the defense team. This started a bloody fight, in the epic style. During the fighting one of the prosecutors spotted Eyjolf, and said to Kari Solmundarson: "There is Eyjolf Bolverksson now in case you want to pay him back for the bracelet!" "I think that is very much in order," Kari said, and hurtled a spear right through the wily defense lawyer.

After the fighting broke up, a settlement was made. The relatives of those killed in the burning house were paid off with *wergild*, or "blood money" and the murderers were banished for three years. The deaths in the courtroom fight were compensated, death for death, and those left over, with *wergild*. The question then arose what to do about the death of the lawyer Eyjolf. The decision was made that nothing was owed for his death, as "he was declared to have fallen on his trickery and perversion of justice."[4]

LOOSE CANONS

The medieval Church inherited the assumptions and methods of Roman law, applied them to teachings of the New Testament and developed Canon law—a creation that would have delighted Cicero and appalled Christ.

Canon law was used in ecclesiastical courts, which had jurisdiction over the clergy, matrimonial cases, disputes over wills, defamation and the like. The descendant of Roman and Canon law today is the civil law system of Europe and South America. Anglo-Saxon law evolved into the common law system of England and the United States.

The following poem, called "Dic Christi Veritas" after its first line, questions whether God's truth can be found in courts or with judges. It is from the *Carmina Burana*, a collection of Latin verses, many of them vulgar, written down at the Monastary of Benedictbeurn at the end of the Thirteenth Century.

Say, truth of Christ,
say, dear rarity,
say, dear charity,
where do you live now?
Is it in the valley of Vision?

Or on the throne of Pharaoh?
Or on high with Nero?
Or in the dark with Timon?
Is it in the bulrush ark
with the weeping Moses?
Or in the house of Romulus,
with the fulminating Edict?

In the fulminating edict,
under a thundering judge,
the summoning into court,
the burdening with sentence,
Truth is oppressed,
torn apart and sold,
Justice prostituting herself.
One goes and returns again,
To the court, Nor does
Anything result,
Until one is stripped
Of his last farthing.[5]

HISTORICAL BRIEF

Call Me Irresponsalis

Norman civil courts required plaintiff and defendant to plead their own cases, but on rare occasions, granted only by royal writ, substitutes could appear. At these times, an attorney, or *responsalis*, represented the absent party. Inevitably, substitution became more and more common, and soon, despite a great deal of resistance, attorneys became a fixture. These attorneys were not officers of the court or a recognized profession, but as early as the Twelfth Century, certain names began to show up suspiciously often. By the Thirteenth Century, the idea that people with disputes had direct access to the tribunals established to resolve them was all over. Lawyers had come to dominate the courts.

The headaches started immediately. In 1240, the Abbot of Ramsey declared that none of his tenants was to bring a pleader into his courts to impede or delay justice. A revealing pronouncement of 1275 threatened imprisonment for the attorney guilty of collusive or deceitful practice. In a record of 1280, the mayor and aldermen of London lamented the ignorance and ill manners of the lawyers who practiced in the civic courts, and promised suspension for any who took money with both hands or reviled an antagonist.[6]

A HYMN TO THOSE ON LOW

The following ditty, originally in Latin, was found in a breviary, apparently of the Thirteenth Century, set to music so as to resemble the hymns:

They shall weep, those labial vendors,
Lawyers, fraud enacting;
Striving more for what law renders
By the suits' protracting,
Than the right exacting.
So the church to consultation
Calls attorneys many;
For, despite this wide vocation,
Moved by equity's inspiration,
She finds hardly any.
Destitute of verity,
Counting lawsuits their subsistence;
Robbing laws of all consistence,
Sacred laws of long existence;
Bound by a retaining fee,
Steeped in vile duplicity.
Deeds of wicked men fomenting;
Working deep iniquity
When they seem to right consenting.
Christ, the Judge, of their repenting
Will not spare falsity.[8]

> **"The three learned professions live by roguery on the three parts of man. The doctor mauls our bodies, the parson starves our soul and the lawyer ensnares our minds."**
>
> English Proverb[7]

JUDGING JUDGES

True Confessions of a Chinese Magistrate

The Chalk Circle is an anonymous Chinese play of the Thirteenth or Fourteenth Century. Chang Hai-T'ang, the good second wife of a wealthy merchant, is falsely accused of murdering her husband by the evil first wife, who is having an affair with a law clerk. The poor Chang Hai-T'ang's conviction seems certain with the help of an ignorant and venal magistrate, Su-Shun. Following the dictates of medieval Chinese drama, the judge introduces himself quite candidly. Were it only that all corrupt judges were as straightforward:

I am the magistrate of the Court of Ch'ing-ch'iu. My
name is Su-Shun.
Although I perform the functions of judge,
I am unacquainted
With a single article of the code.
I love but one thing:
With his death has flown

The clink of silver;
Graced with his beauteous
White metal,
The pleader is sure to win his case.[9]

BARTOLUS AND THE BASTARDS

Bartolus de Saxoferrato (c. 1313-1357), was a child prodigy who degenerated into one of the great law professors of the Middle Ages. He was already teaching law at the age of twenty-six and his writings dominated legal thinking for two centuries. The Holy Roman Emperor Charles IV ennobled Bartolus and also granted him an unusual privilege. He decreed that the jurist should have the right to legitimize any child born out of wedlock who attended his law courses. Apparently, the Emperor was one of the first to recognize that law school was an appropriate place for bastards.[10]

LEGAL LYRICS

Langland Lambasts Lawyers

Because not many people in the Middle Ages could write, and those who could were either rich and powerful or patronized by the rich and powerful, the view of the commoner was seldom expressed. An exception was the record left by the medieval English poet William Langland (c. 1330-1400) who remained a poor clerk his whole life. He wrote *The Vision of William concerning Piers Plowman*, an allegorical look at the England of his day, warts and all. Indeed, he considered lawyers and courts a warty subject:

Yet stood there scores of men in scarves of silk—
Law sergeants they seemed who served in court,
Pleaded cases for pennies and impounded the law,
And not for love of our Lord unloosed their lips once:
You might better measure mist on Malvern Hills
Than get a "mum" from their lips till money is showed.[11]

Later on in his work, Langland warns:

Ye lawyers, ye advocates, be sure of this:
When ye draw near to death and pray for pardon,
Your pardon at your parting hence will be but small.[12]

"The Jews ruin themselves at the Passover, the Moors at their marriages and the Christians in their lawsuits."

Medieval Spanish Proverb[13]

THE LABYRINTH OF LEGAL LANGUAGE

Oyez, Oyez, Oy Vey

In the late Middle Ages, the English courts used "law French" in all proceedings— a garbled version of bad Latin and bastardized French. The use of Latin had its roots in the legal system adopted from the Romans, and the French usage originated when that tongue became the language of English government after the Norman conquest. Outside of the courtroom, however, no one spoke or understood this hybrid tongue. This resulted in the strange spectacle of defendants, plaintiffs, witnesses and juries engaging in proceedings in which they hadn't the slightest inkling of what was happening. Finally, in 1362, in the reign of Edward III, a statute directed that English be used in all legal proceedings.

The statute, of course, was written in French.[14]

KEEPING LAWYERS OUT OF TROUBLE

A statute of 1362 prohibited lawyers from sitting in Parliament because of their interest and activity in stirring up lawsuits. Again, in 1404, lawyers were forbidden to take seats in that body by a writ of King Henry IV.[15]

THE LAWYER IS CALLED HOME

In the folktales, songs and stories of different cultures, the Devil and the lawyer crop up together uncommonly often— sometimes jousting, more often boon companions. This one from the England of the Middle Ages not only recounts an adventure of the pair, but also attests to the great depth of feeling which the populace held for the attorney:

A certain man was a lawyer of different towns, pitiless, grasping, and making great exactions from all in his power. On a certain day, when, for the purpose of exacting tribute, he was hastening to a certain town, the Devil, in the likeness of a man, joined him on his journey; whom, as well from the horror which he felt as from their conversation, he perceived to be the evil one. He greatly feared to go with him; but in no way, either by praying, or by making the sign of the cross, could he shake him off.

As they walked on together, a certain poor man approached them, leading a pig by a string. And as the pig ran hither and thither, the angry man cried out, "Devil take thee!" Hearing this, the lawyer, hoping that by this means he could free himself from his companion, said to him, "Listen, friend, that pig is given to thee; go, seize him." The fiend responded, "He is not given to me from the heart, and so I cannot take him."

Then, as they were passing through another place, a baby cried; and its mother, standing in the door of her house, exclaimed, in a petulant tone, "Devil take thee! Why dost thou trouble me with thy crying?" Then the lawyer said, "See, you are the richer by one soul; take the baby, which is yours." To whom the the Devil, as before, said, "It is not given to me from the heart, but such is the way of speaking that people have when they are angry."

But as they began to draw near to the town to which they were bound, some men, seeing them afar off from the town, and knowing the occasion of the lawyer's coming, cried out, "Devil take thee, and go to the Devil!" Hearing this, the fiend, wagging his head and laughing, said to the lawyer, "Behold, they have given thee to me from the bottom of their hearts; and therefore thou art mine." And the Devil seized him that very hour, but what he did with him is not known.[16]

LEGAL LYRICS

Wasted Haste

Lawyers are famous for their frenzied running about, and more than one layperson has suspected this habit is more for the sake of appearance than necessity. This is how Geoffrey Chaucer (1340-1400), described a "Man of Lawe" in the prologue to *Canterbury Tales:*

> *No-wher so bisy a man as he ther n'as*
> *And yet he semed bisier than he was.*[17]

A PATRONIZING DISCOVERY

The Catholic Church used to assign patron saints to various localities and professions. St. Evona, or St. Yves, a *breton* attorney, was made the patron saint of lawyers. In the words of an old folk rhyme, Yves was sanctified because he was: "A lawyer but not a thief. Such a thing is beyond belief." Some people, though, as this tale narrated by the Seventeenth Century writer William Carr indicates, believed that another patron might have been more appropriate:

> St. Evona . . . came to Rome to Entreat the Pope to give the Lawyers of Brittanie a Patron, to which the Pope replied that he knew of no saint but was disposed of to other professions, at which Evona was very sad and earnestly beg'd the Pope to think of one for them: at last the Pope proposed to St. Evona that he should goe round the Church of St. John de Latera blindfould and after he had said so many Ave Marias, that the first Saint he laid hold of should be his patron, which the good old lawyer willingly undertook, and at the end of his Ave Marias, he stopt at St. Michel's Altar, where he layd hold of the Divell, under St. Michel's feet, and cryd out, "this is our Saint, let him be our Patron."

> . . . seeing what a Patron he had chosen, he went to his lodgings so dejected, that in a few moneths after he died, and coming to heaven's gates knockt hard. Whereupon St. Peter asked who it was that knockt so boudly. He replyed that he was St. Evona, the Advocate.

> "Away, away," said St. Peter; "there is but one Advocate in heaven; here is no room for you Lawyers."

> "But," said St. Evona, "I am that honest Lawyer who never took fees on both sides, or pleaded in a bad cause, nor did I ever set my Naibours together by the Eares, or lived by the sins of the people."

> "Well, then," said St. Peter, "come in."[18]

HE WASN'T JUST PLAYING AROUND

Jack Cade is well known as the Shakespearean character who, in tandem with Dick the Butcher, voices that immortal sentiment: "The first thing we do, let's kill all the lawyers." Shakespeare's fictional figure is based on a real Jack Cade, an English soldier who led a Fifteenth Century revolt against the political, economic and legal abuses of the Crown and its administrators. With some 20,000 followers, he succeeded in occupying London and beheading a particularly venal royal minister, but the revolt was soon suppressed and Cade killed, without any lasting reforms achieved. Although Shakespeare lampooned Cade, the real article did have sentiments in common with his fictional namesake:

> *The law serveth as naught else in these days but for to do wrong, for nothing is sped but false matters by color of the law for mede, drede and favor.*[19]

PRINCIPLES? WHAT PRINCIPLES?

Sir John Fortescu (c.1394-c.1476) was a Lord Chancellor and the author of an early law text, *De Laudibus Legum Angliae*, (*In Praise of the Laws of England*). That he had much to praise in the equivocations of the law is shown by this anecdote:

> *When Lord Chancellor during the War of the Roses, Sir John Fortescu wrote a treatise to support, on principles of constitutional law, the claim of the House of Lancaster to the crown. But when Edward [who was from the House of York] was firmly established on the throne, Sir John expressed his willingness to submit himself to the reigning monarch. Edward, with some malice, required that, as a condition of his pardon, he must write another treatise upon the disputed question of the succession in support of the claim of the House of York against the House of Lancaster.*[20]

The old lawyer had no difficulty complying, thus exhibiting a lawyering skill still abused today: He could support either side with equal enthusiasm.

LESS IS MORE

Another famous anti-lawyer thinker of the Middle Ages was Sir (later Saint) Thomas More (1478-1535). He studied law, but by the time he wrote *Utopia*, published in 1516, which described his best of all possible worlds, he did not have much use for the legal cabal. He wrote that in Utopia:

> *. . . they utterly exclude and banish all attorneys, proctors, and serjeants-at-law, which craftily handle matters, and subtly dispute of the laws. For they think it proper that every man should plead his own matter, and tell the same tale before the judge that he would tell to his lawyer. So shall there be less circumstance of words, and the truth shall sooner come to light, while the judge, with a discrete judgement weighs the words of him whom no lawyer has instructed with deceit, and helps and bears out simple folk against the false and malicious circumventions of crafty lawyers. This is hard to observe in other countries, so infinite the number of blind and intricate laws. But in Utopia every man is*

*learned in law. For (as I said) they have very few laws,
and the plainer and clearer that any interpretation is,
that one they allow as most just. For all laws, say they,
be made and published only to the intent that by them
every man should be put in remembrance of his duty.
But the crafty and subtle interpretation of them (for as
much as few can attain thereto) can put very few in
that remembrance, where as the simple, the plain, and
clear meaning of the laws is open to every man.*[21]

HERE I STAND, I CAN DO NO OTHER

Martin Luther (1483-1546), was studying law at the University of Erfurt when his religous epiphany led him to abruptly abandon his secular studies and enter a monastery. (Perhaps more law students would do well to follow Luther's fine example.) After he became the leading religious reformer in Europe, he wrote:

*God has not given laws to make out of right wrong, and
out of wrong right, as the un-Christianlike lawyers do,
who study law only for the sake of gain and profit.*[22]

NOTES

1   Malalas 384. From A.H.M. Jones, *Later Roman Empire*, Johns Hopkins University Press, Baltimore, 1986, pg. 494.

2   *Codex Justinianus* III 1.13.530. Translated by J. Roth.

3   René A. Wormser, *The Story of the Law*, Simon & Schuster, New York, 1962, pg. 234.

4   *Njal's Saga*, Penguin Books, New York, 1960, Chapters 138-45. Translated by Magnus Magnusson and Hermann Palsson; *Njal's Saga*, New York University Press, New York, 1955. Translated by Carl F. Bayerschmidt and Lee M. Hollander.

5   *Carmina Burana* XCIII, pg. 51. Translated by J. Roth.

6   Sir Frederick Pollock and Frederic W. Maitland, *The History of the English Law before the Time of Edward I,* Cambridge University Press, Cambridge,1968, pgs. 215-16.

7   Selwyn G. Champion, *Racial Proverbs: A Selection of the World's Proverbs arranged Linguistically*, Barnes and Noble, New York, 1950, pg. 33.

8   Irving Browne, *Law and Lawyers in Literature*, Soule and Bugbee, Boston, 1883 (reprinted by Wm. W. Gaunt & Sons, Inc., Holmes Beach, Florida, 1982), pgs. 124-25.

9   Anonymous, *The Chalk Circle*, Act II, from *Poetic Drama*, Alfred Kreymborg (ed.), Modern Age Books, New York, 1941, pg. 158. Translated by Ethel van der Veer.

10 Cecil N. Sidney Woolf, *Bartolus of Sassoferrato*, Cambridge University Press, *passim*.

11 William Landland, *The Vision of William concerning Piers Plowman*, Prologue 210-215, from M.H. Abrams (ed.), *The Norton Anthology of English Literature*, W.W. Norton, New York, 1979, pg. 333. Translated by E. Talbot Donaldson.

12 Langland, *Piers Plowman*, ll. 1332-1400.

13 Champion, *Racial Proverbs*, pg. 303.

14 Charles Rembar, *The Law of the Land: The Evolution of Our Legal System*, Simon & Schuster, New York, 1980, pg. 178.

15 Charles Warren, *A History of the American Bar*, Little, Brown and Co., Boston, 1911 (reprinted by William S. Hein, Buffalo N.Y., 1980), pg. 25.

16 Browne, *Law and Lawyers in Literature*, pgs. 301-2.

17 Geoffrey Chaucer, *Canterbury Tales*, Prologue ll. 321-22; from Walter K. Skeat (ed.), *The Student's Chaucer,* Oxford, London, 1929, pg. 423.

18 William Carr (1688) in Robert E. Megarry, *2nd Miscellany-at-Law*, Stevens & Sons, London, 1973, pgs. 41-2.

19   Warren, *A History of the American Bar*, pg. 26.

20   L. J. Bigelow, *Bench and Bar: A Complete Digest of the Wit, Humor, Asperities, and Amenities of the Law,* Harper & Brothers, New York, 1871, pg. 33.

21   Sir Thomas More, *Utopia,*. Adapted from the translation by Ralph Robinson, 1556; reprinted in London, 1869, pg. 128.

22   In *Table-Talk* 830 (1569) from H.L. Mencken, *A New Dictionary of Quotations on Historical Principles*, Alfred E. Knopf, New York, 1942, pg. 666.

CHAPTER THREE

THE
SIXTEENTH &
SEVENTEENTH
CENTURIES

HISTORICAL BRIEF

Too Much of a Bad Thing

For many tortuous centuries, the law and the courts of England grew unrestrained—a hodgepodge of historical accident, capricious whim, political manuevering and archaic tradition raveled together without rhyme or rationale. By the Sixteenth Century, the British citizen staggered amidst a sprawling, lumbering and confusing legal system. Myriad courts functioned simultaneously with ill-defined and overlapping jurisdictions, different procedure and independent court personnel. There were local courts, Chancery Courts, the Star Chamber, the Court of Common Pleas, the Court of Wards and Liveries, Admiralty Court, the King's Bench, the Court of Request. And more.

All kinds of law evolved to be practiced and malpracticed in these far-flung courts: the common law, ecclesiastical law, the law of the sea, the law of equity. And more.

And of course, to guide the guileless through this Chinese puzzle, there were lawyers. Lawyers in bewildering, stunning variety: attorneys, serjeants-at-law, apprentices, prothonotaries, pleaders, filazers, solicitors, utter-barristers and inner-barristers. And still more. Some could practice in all courts, some could practice in some but not others, some in only one, some never saw a courtroom inside or out; some had training, others none; some only wrote, some only pleaded; some considered it unseemly to have contact with a client, others were out groping for business at every fair and market. Scholars are still rummaging about in the dusty writs left behind, trying to make sense of it all.

SHIELDING A NEW WORLD FROM AN OLD WORLD PLAGUE

Bernal Diaz, a conquistador turned chronicler, reported that the first law passed in Portabelo, Panama (founded by the Spanish around 1530) asked the King of Spain to bar all lawyers from immigrating to the New World "because where they go, trouble soon follows." The decree was granted, but judging from the present state of affairs, there must have been a loophole.

The essayist Michel de Montaigne reported that King Ferdinand, sending colonists to the West Indies, "wisely provided that they should not carry along with them any law students, for fear lest suits should get a footing in that new world; as being a science in its own nature the mother of alteration and division; judging with Plato, that lawyers and physicians are the pests of a country."[1]

"In a thousand pounds of law there's not an ounce of love."

English Proverb[2]

THE LABYRINTH OF LEGAL LANGUAGE

Perpetuating Perplexities

Before 1540, landowners did not usually have any right to decide what would happen to their land upon their death. Only movable property could be bequeathed by a will. In most cases, all land went to the eldest son, prodigal or not. The Statute of Wills, passed in Henry VIII's reign, for the first time allowed land to be disposed of by will. Lawyers had a field day—immediately setting to work to devise ingenious ways to keep the wealth in the hands of the wealthy by putting land into practically perpetual ownership using wills. To stop this legal abuse, the Rule against Perpetuities was promptly passed. To this day, this nearly incomprehensible rule is the bane of law students:

> *The vesting of a future interest may not be postponed for a longer period than a life or any number of lives in being (including the life of a person en ventre sa mere at the time of the limitation) and twenty-one years after the dropping of life or if there are several lives after the dropping of the last surviving life; but at the end of this period the limitation may still take effect if the person in whom the interest is to vest is en ventre sa mere.*[3]

Even though the rule is useless, law schools continue to offer entire courses on it—apparently on the theory that no one is fit to be a lawyer who has not been tortured by its meaningless complexities. Instructors who teach bar review courses, one of the few places in legal education where the practical is emphasized, advise skipping over any question on the rule that shows up on the bar exam. It's too convoluted. Even for lawyers.

THEY'RE NOT HAVING FUN, YET...

Among men of the learned professions, a most self-satisfied group of men, the lawyers, may hold themselves in the highest esteem. For while they laboriously roll up the stone of Sisyphus by the force of weaving six hundred laws together at the same time, by stacking commentary on commentary and opinion on opinion regardless of how far removed from the purpose, they continue to make their profession seem to be the most difficult of all. What is actually tedious they consider brilliant.

Desiderius Erasmus (c. 1466-1536),
Swiss-German humanist[4]

MONTAIGNE'S CONVICTIONS

Michel Eyquem, the Seignor de Montaigne (1533-1592), studied law, but never practiced it. He became a judge, though it owed more to his noble birth than to anything he had learned about legal procedure. He did learn about lawyers, however, and his experience brought him to the following conclusions:

There's no reason why a lawyer or a banker should not recognize the knavery that is part of his vocation. An honest man is not responsible for the vices or the stupidity of his calling, and need not refuse to practice them. They are customs of his country and there is profit in them.[5]

and

What can be more outrageous than to see a nation where, by lawful custom, the office of a judge is to be bought and sold, where judgments are paid for with ready money, and where justice may legally be denied to him that has not wherewithal to pay; where this merchandise is in so great repute, as in our government, to furnish a fourth estate of wrangling lawyers, to add to the three ancient ones of the church, nobility, and the people.[6]

LEGAL LYRICS

The voyce of the last Trumpet, blowen by the seventh Angel (as is mentioned in the eleventh of the Apocalips), callying al estate of men to the ryght path of theyr vocation; wherein are conteyned xii lessons to twelve severall estats of men; which, if they learne and folowe, al shall be wel, and nothing amis is the forbidding, but essentially optimistic title of a book written by Robert Crowley and printed in London in 1550. As the title makes unclear, it contains moral lessons and admonitions to, among others, beggars, lewd priests and lawyers. The following is a portion of "The Lawiar's Lesson:"

But now I call the to repent,
And thy greedines to forsake;
For God's wrath is agaynst the bent,
If thou wilt not my warnyng take.
Fyrst, call unto thy memorye
For what cause the Laws wer fyrst made;
And then apply the busily
To the same ende to use thy trade.
The Lawes were made, undoubtedly,
That al such men as are oppreste,
Myght in the same fynde remedy,
And leade their lyves in quiet reste.
Dost thou then walke in thy callying?
When for to vexe the innocent
Thou wilt stande at a barre, ballyng,
Wyth all the craft thou canst invente.
I says ballyng—for better name
To have it cannot be worthye;
When lyke a beast, without al shame,
Thou wilt do wrong to get money.[7]

LENGTHY BRIEFS

Thomas Egerton was Lord Chancellor of Britain from 1603 to 1617, and apparently a man with a rare sense of justice. When attorney Richard Mylward drew up a replication [plaintiff's answer to a defendant's plea] of 120 pages, the Lord Chancellor thought the job should have been done in sixteen. He prescribed the following penalty:

It is therefore ordered that the warden of the Fleet shall take the said Richard Mylward . . . into his custody, and shall bring him unto Westminster Hall on Saturday next . . . and there and then shall cut a hole in the myddest

*of the same engrossed replication . . . and put the said
Richard's head through the same hole, and so let the
same replication hang about his shoulders with the
written side outward; and then, the same so hanging,
shall lead the same Richard, bare headed and bare
faced, round Westminster Hall, whilst the courts are
sitting, and shall shew him at the bar of every of the
three courts within the Hall.*[9]

THE EVER-WAXING BAR

In 1560, there was one attorney for every 20,000 people in
England; in 1606, there was one for every 4,000; and in 1640,
one for every 2,500.[10]

No statistics recorded a proportionate increase in justice.

SELECTIONS FROM A MASTER

William Shakespeare (1564-1616)

Shakespeare knew the legal system of his day quite well—
and his experiences were not pleasant ones. When he was
thirteen or fourteen, his father was involved in extended
litigation that contributed to a serious decline in the family's
fortunes. Surviving documents mention that a suit was brought
against Shakespeare in 1596, he sued someone in 1609 and gave
a sworn statement in a lawsuit in 1612. Shakespeare's involve-
ment with lawyers, judges and courts was probably much more
extensive than the few remaining documents indicate and his
plays show that his opinion of the whole legal profession was
none too high.

King Lear

In Act I, Scene 4, Lear, the Earl of Kent and the Fool are
talking in the Duke of Albany's palace:

Fool: *Sirrah, I'll teach thee a speech.*

Lear: *Do.*

Fool: *Mark it, nuncle:*
Have more than thou showest,
Speak less than thou knowest,
Lend less than thou owest,
Ride more than thou goest,
Learn more than thou trowest,
Set less than thou throwest;

Leave thy drink and thy whore,
And keep in-a-door,
And thou shalt have more
Than two tens to a score.

Kent: *This is nothing, fool.*

Fool: *Then 'tis like the breath of an unfee'd lawyer, you*
gave me nothing for 't. Can you make no use of
nothing, nuncle?

Lear: *Why, no, boy; nothing can be made out of*
nothing.

Henry VI, Part 2

In Act IV, Scene 2, lies Shakespeare's most famous line on lawyers—possibly the best known of all of history's indictments of the legal tribe. Jack Cade is leading a Peasants' Revolt, to which the playwright is less than sympathetic, and is giving a speech outlining the utopia he will institute when he becomes king. Dick the Butcher is in the crowd:

Cade: *Be brave, then; for your captain is brave, and*
vows reformation. There shall be in England seven
halfpenny loaves sold for a penny; the three-hooped pot
shall have ten hoops; and I will make it a felony to drink
small beer: all the realm shall be in common; and in
Cheapside shall my palfry go to grass: and when I am
king, as king I will be—

All: *God save your majesty!*

Cade: *I thank you, good people; there shall be no*
money; all shall eat and drink on my score; and I will
apparel them all in one livery, that they may agree like
brothers and worship me as their lord.

Dick: *The first thing we do, let's kill all the lawyers.*

Cade: *Nay, that I mean to do. Is not this a lamentable*
thing, that of the skin of an innocent lamb should be
made parchment? that parchment, being scribbled o'er,
should undo a man? Some say the bee stings: but I say,
'tis the bee's wax; for I did but seal once to a thing, and
I was never mine own man since. How now! who's
there?

A lawyer is brought in, and true to his word, Cade has him hanged "with his pen and ink-horn around his neck."

Hamlet

The best-known skull in the graveyard scene (Act V, Scene 1) is that of Yorick the jester, but an ex-attorney also makes an appearance. Hamlet and Horatio are watching two gravediggers at work:

> **Hamlet**: *There's another: why may not that be the skull of a lawyer? Where be his quiddities now, his quillities, his cases, his tenures, and his tricks? Why does he suffer this mad knave now to knock him about the sconce with a dirty shovel, and will not tell him of his action of battery? Hum! This fellow might in's time a great buyer of land, with his statutes, his recognizances, his fines, his double vouchers, his recoveries: is this the fine of his fines, and the recovery of his recoveries, to have his fine pate full of fine dirt? Will his vouchers vouch him no more of his purchases, and double ones too, than the length and breadth of a pair of indentures? The very conveyances of his lands will scarcely lie in this box; and must the inheritor himself have no more, ha?*

> **Horatio**: *Not a jot more, my lord.*

> **Hamlet**: *Is not parchment made of sheep-skins?*

> **Horatio**: *Ay, my lord, and of calf-skins too.*

> **Hamlet**: *They are sheep and calves which seek out assurance in that . . .*

LEGAL LYRICS

Another Sixteenth Century playwright, Christopher Marlowe (1564-1593), wrote *The Tragical History of of the Life and Death of Doctor Faustus*, which was published posthumuously in 1604. In the first scene, trying to fix on a subject worthy of his great intellect, Faust first calls for Justinian's *Institutes*, an important textbook of law at the time. After tossing off some Latin legalese, he wisely rejects the lawyerly path:

> *This study fits a mercenary drudge,*
> *Who aims at nothing but external trash,*
> *Too servile and illiberal for me.*[11]

"The Isle of Wight has no monks, lawyers, or foxes."

English Proverb[12]

JUST SAY NO

The English poet and epigrammist Francis Quarles (1592-1644), had this prosaic advice for laypeople:

Use law and physic only in cases of necessity; they that use them otherwise, abuse themselves into weak bodies and light purses; they are good remedies, bad recreations, but ruinous habits.[13]

ABYSMAL ATTORNEYS-GENERAL

Sir Edward Coke (1552-1634), is best known for his work, published in 1628, with the imposing title *The First Part of the Institutes of the Laws of England or a Commentary upon Littleton.* Coke called Littleton's writings "the most perfect and absolute work that was written in any humane science;" a contemporary jurist called it a "clumsy, disorderly, senseless piece of jargon." In 1598, to secure an alliance with the ruling party, Coke married Lady Elizabeth Hatton in a private house. This was contrary to canon law, and Coke was prosecuted. He managed to obtain a dispensation by successfully pleading, of all things, ignorance of the law.

Coke had a distinguished legal career, becoming Solicitor-General, then Attorney-General in 1593, Chief Justice of Common Pleas in 1606 and Chief Justice of the King's Bench in 1613. Much of Coke's success was due to his willingness, as both attorney and judge, to carry out the King's repression of reform through the courts. As Attorney-General, he prosecuted Sir Walter Raleigh on a trumped-up charge of treason.

Coke's conduct of the trial—covering up the lack of evidence with vicious and unsubstantiated attacks—is hardly a credit to a man thought of as one of the founders of modern law. Lord Mansfield said of it, one hundred years later: "I would not have made Coke's speech in Sir Walter Raleigh's case to gain all Coke's estate and reputation." This exchange is typical of Coke's "cross-examination" of Raleigh:

Coke*: You are the absolutest traitor that ever was.*

Raleigh*: Your words will not prove it.*

And later:

Coke*: Thou art the most vile and execrable traitor that ever lived.*

Raleigh*: You speak indiscreetly, uncivilly, and barbarously.*

Coke*: I want words sufficient to express thy viperous treasons.*

Raleigh*: I think you want words indeed, for you have spoken one thing half a dozen times.*

Based on this type of brilliant and logical argumentation by the great legal scholar Coke, Raleigh was convicted and sentenced to death. His death sentence was commuted to imprisonment. Raleigh was later released, only to be hanged a few years later for crimes committed on an expedition to South America. Coke himself ended up in prison for seven months in 1621, but came to a happier end, dying peacefully at the age of 82.[14]

> *"I wish the law written in one vulgar language; for now it is an old mixt and corrupt language only understood by lawyers."*
>
> James I (1566-1625), King of England and Scotland[15]

LEGAL LYRICS

The Woes of the Weal

Bishop Joseph Hall (1574-1656), was a churchman, ambassador, poet, playwright and prose writer. Obviously, a very learned man. And he didn't like lawyers. Here are his thoughts on the subject, in rhyme:

> *Woe to the weal where many lawyers be,*
> *For there is sure much store of malady.*
> *'Twas truly said, and truly was foreseen,*
> *The fat kine are devoured of the lean. . .*
>
> *The crouching client, with low bended knee,*
> *And many worships, and fair flattery,*
> *Tells on his tale as smoothly as him list,*
> *But still the lawyer's eye squints on his fist;*
> *If that seem lined with a larger fee,*
> *Doubt not the suit, the law is plain for thee.*
> *Tho' must he buy his vainer hope with price,*
> *Dishclout his crowns, and thank him for advice.*[16]

ESQ., R.I.P.

> *He professed the lawe. Yet he embraced*
> *Peace and abhored bribes and faveors*

Epitaph of lawyer James Mott of Norfolk[17]

UNSLOPPY COPYING

Most legal proceedings of this time involved no oral arguments, but were instead exchanges of written pleadings. Legal proceedings generated mountains—verily, mountain ranges—of complaints, pleas, answers, demurrers, briefs, exceptions, replies and other such documents. No problem— lawyers charged by the page. Complained a writer in 1647: "I did see an answer . . . of forty of their sheets which [recopied in normal writing] was brought down to six sheets."[18]

THE ANATOMY OF MELANCHOLY

We may justly tax our wrangling lawyers, they do consenescere in litibus (grow old in lawsuits], are so litigious and here on earth, that I think they will plead their clients' causes hereafter, some of them in hell.

Robert Burton (1577-1640), English scholar[19]

ROGUES GALLERY

Sir Francis Bacon (1561-1626)

Bacon was born in London in 1561. He began studying law when he was eighteen and soon became one of the most successful lawyers of his time. He entered Parliament in 1584, served several terms, and rose—or fell, depending on your point of view—to the bench in 1586.

Although a wealthy man, Bacon found it difficult to live within his means, and was, as a result, always seeking wealthy patrons. One of them was Lord Essex, who managed to get Bacon appointed as "Queen's Counsel Learned in the Law." Essex also gave Bacon an estate, but when his patron fell from grace and was accused of treason, Bacon helped prepare the prosecution's case against his old friend and benefactor. Bacon even wrote a public exposition of Essex's supposed crimes.

Bacon replaced Coke as Attorney-General in 1613. He was quite enthusiastic about his job. One of his cases was against Reverend Peacham, a Puritan clergyman, who was accused of treason after criticizing the King. In his report on the investigation, in 1614, Bacon wrote:

Peacham was examined before torture, in torture, and after torture, nothing could be drawn from him, he still persisting in his obstinate and inexcusable denials and former answers.[20]

In another context, Bacon observed: "Judges must beware of hard constructions and strained inferences, for there is no worse torture than the torture of laws." One doubts whether the Reverend Peacham would have agreed.

Despite his inquisitorial techniques, Bacon was unsure of getting Peacham convicted and approached each member of the King's bench privately for guidance on how to ensure the result. When he asked Coke, he was told, in Shakespearean English, to take a hike. He then simply had the trial transferred from the King's Court to the Court of the Lord Chief Baron and obtained a conviction.

King James finally discharged Coke as Chief Justice. Bacon was rewarded for his toadyism, appointed to the Privy Council in 1616 and made Lord Chancellor in 1618. In this post, he became Baron Verulam, and finally Viscount St. Albans. One historian wrote: "The years during which he held the Chancellorship were the most disgraceful years of a disgraceful reign . . . and above all in the attempt to coerce the judges into prostrating law at the King's feet he took a personal part."[21]

In 1621, there was a raging controversy in Parliament about granting monopolies, and in the midst of it the information came out that Bacon had been taking bribes in connection with the grants. Bacon immediately confessed: "I am guilty of corruption and do renounce all defense." But he did offer an ingenious excuse, reportedly explaining: "I was careful to take bribes from both sides so that tainted money would never affect my decision." He was fined 40,000 pounds, imprisoned and restrained from holding further office. However, the King, in view of services rendered, remitted his imprisonment and reassigned the fine. He even granted Bacon a pension of 1,000 pounds a year.

After his fall, Bacon devoted himself to writing and to scientific experiments. He died on April 9, 1626, from pneumonia caught while performing one of those experiments—trying to preserve a chicken by stuffing it with snow.[22]

COLONIAL AMERICA RESISTS EUROPEAN LAWYERDOM

"Nothing in the early legal history of the Colonies is more striking," wrote historian Charles Warren, "than the uniformly low position held in the community by the members of the legal profession."[23] Daniel Boorstin declared of this period: "Distrust of lawyers became an institution."[24] From Massachusetts to Georgia, our intrepid foreparents despised lawyers and did their best to keep them out. Alas, unsuccessfully.

The religous communities of New England, with Puritan traditions, as well as the Quaker communities in Pennsylvania and the Dutch settlements in New York, rectified most problems informally. Sometimes, of course, a dispute proved impossible to settle by "talking it out"—even under the guidance of clergy. In these cases, formal mediation techniques, similar to those becoming more popular today, were often used.

From an early date, the Quakers appointed three "peacemakers" in every precinct for binding arbitration. Later, the Quakers encouraged those litigating in court to choose referees by mutual consent, whose decision would have the same effect as a jury verdict. Quite a large number of the disputes in the Pennsylvania colony were settled this way.[25] A 1635 Boston town meeting ordered that no congregation member could litigate before trying arbitration, and Reverend John Cotton, the leading Puritan minister of the time, stated that to sue a fellow church member was a "defect in brotherly love."

Desperate to check what they considered an Old World plague, the Colonies passed a great deal of anti-lawyer legislation.

In 1641, the "Body of Liberties" adopted by the Massachusetts Bay Colony prohibited all freemen from being represented by a paid attorney:

Every man that findeth himselfe unfit to plead his own cause in any court shall have libertie to employ any man against whom the court doth not except, to help him, Provided he give noe fee or reward for his pains.[26]

In Virginia, in 1645:

Whereas many troublesom suits are multiplied by the unskilfulness and covetousness of attorneys who have more intended their own profit and their inordinate lucre than the good and benefit of their clients, be it therefore enacted that all mercenary attorneys be wholly expelled from such office.[27]

In South Carolina, in 1667:

It shall be a base and vile thing to plead for money or reward; nor shall anyone . . . be permitted to plead another man's cause, till, before the judge in open court, he hath taken an oath, that he doth not plead for money or reward, nor hath nor will receive nor directly nor indirectly bargained with the party, whose cause he is going to plead, for money or any other reward for pleading his cause.[28]

There was a ban in Connecticut too, and in fact, in that colony, as late as 1698, lawyers were classed in one law with drunkards and keepers of disorderly houses.[29] In Pennsylvania, it was said: "They have no lawyers. Everyone is to tell his own case, or some friend for him . . . 'Tis a happy country." [30]

LAWYERLESS NEW WORLD

The Colonies' First Lawyer and the Reception He Received

The very first lawyer to arrive and practice in the Colonies was Thomas Morton, who came to Massachusetts in 1625. Governor Bradford described him as "a kind of pettie-fogger of Furnewells Inne"—that is, a cheat from one of the inferior Inns of Chancery in England. Governor Dudley called him "insolent." He didn't last long. He was jailed for scandalous behavior and shipped out of the Colony post haste.[31]

The Colonies' Second Lawyer and the Distinction He Received

The next to give it a go in the New World was Thomas Lechford. He arrived in Boston in 1637 or 1638. It is often said that there is plenty of work for two lawyers where there is none for one, and Lechford found little recompense in blustering and sputtering with himself: A smarter lawyer would have brought along a colleague. Lechford soon got in trouble with the authorities. In 1639, he received the distinction of becoming the first American lawyer to be disbarred—"debarred from pleading any main cause hereafter unless his own and admonished not to presume to meddle. . . ." Of course, it is too basic a contradiction for a lawyer to presume not to meddle, and under this impossible constraint, Lechford soon gave up and sailed back to England. [33]

UTOPIA: LAWYERS NEED NOT APPLY

England in the last half of the Seventeenth Century was "a world turned upside down." Civil wars, Cromwell's Commonwealth and the Puritan Revolution unleashed a torrent of radical religious and political thought. Thousands of soldiers, artisans, farmers and others, rallying around the flags of hundreds of sects such as the Levellers, the Ranters and others, demanded reform, revolution and even Utopia. It is difficult to pin down any unwavering beliefs held by these groups in the swirling currents of the time, but a great many were communalist, anti-clerical and anti-aristocratic. Despite many fierce differences though, they all had one thing in common. As Frank and Fritzie Manuel, authors of *Utopian Thought in the Western World*, report:

> *Utopians differed about precisely who in England was to be included in the category of chosen people, and only*

"Most men are allured to the trade of law, grounding their purposes not on the prudent and heavenly contemplation of justice and equity which was never taught them, but on the promising and pleasing thought of litigious terms, fat contentions and flowing fees."

John Milton
(1608-1674),
English poet [32]

[Gerrard] Winstanly and the Ranters were ready to embrace all Englishmen to full membership in the commonwealth. Even the Levellers excluded servants, beggars, and sometimes wage-earners who had masters. Two classes in society enjoyed universal contempt as worthless, lawyers and university scholars.[34]

THE LABYRINTH OF LEGAL LANGUAGE

Puritan Ethics

Richard Overton, a prominent Leveller, wrote *An Appeal from the Degenerate Representative Body* in July of 1647. In it, he demanded that laws be written in clear, understandable English.

That all Lawes of the Land (lockt up from common capacities in the Latine or French tongues,) may bee translated into the English tongues. And that all records, Orders, Processes, Writs, and other proceedings whatsoever, may all be entered and issued forth in the English tongue, and that in most plaine and common Character used in the Land, commonly called Roman, or Secretary, and that without all or any Latine or French Phrases or Tearmes, and also without all or any abbreviations or abridgement of words, that so the meanest English Commoner that can but read written hand in his owne tongue, may fully understand his owne proceedings in the Law. [35]

The struggle continues.

DIG IT

Gerrard Winstanly was one of the leaders of the Diggers, an offshoot of the Levellers. In his work entitled *The New Law of Righteousness*, published in 1649, Winstanly wrote:

The sentence lies many times in the breast of the judge and not in the letter of the law.

and

And so though the laws be good, yet if they be left to the will of a judge to interpret, the execution hath many time proved bad.

and

And that man who takes upon him to interpret the law doth either darken the sense of the law, or else puts another meaning upon it; and so lifts himself above the Parliament, above the law and above all people in the land.[36]

THE LAWYERS TAKE REVENGE

If the radical critics of the lawyers thought the establishment of the English Commonwealth in 1649 would mean the end of the scourge of the bar, they were disappointed. The lawyers exchanged Royalist scarlet for Republican buff, and continued making money, as is indicated in the following ditty, taken from *An Almanack and Prognostication for the Year 1659*:

> *Behold the learned lawyers! void o'th fears,*
> *Of fifty one, and the two succeeding years,*
> *Have lined their Crowns, and made them pistol proof,*
> *And Magna Charta clad in Coat of Buff,*
> *And with a bolder confidence can take,*
> *A larger fee, for Reformation sake.*[37]

BEDTIME READING

Just a few of the books and tracts popular in London in the Seventeenth Century that give us an idea of the lawyer's reputation at the time:

A Rod for Lawyers Who are Hereby declared Robbers and Deceivers of the Nation;

Essay Wherein is Described the Lawyers, Smugglers and Officers Frauds;

The Downfall of Lawyers;

England's Balme, or Proposals by way of Grievance and Remedy towards the Regulation of Law and Better Administration of Justice;

Perspicuous Compendium of Several Irregularities and Abuses in Present Practice of Common Laws of England;

Sagrir: or Doomes-day drawing nigh, With Thunder and With Lightening to Lawyers, In an Alarum for New Laws, and the Peoples Liberties from the Norman and Babylonian Yokes, Making Discoveries of the present ungodly Laws and Lawyers of the fourth Monarchy.[39]

"The law as it is now constituted serves only to maintain the lawyers and to encourage the rich to oppress the poor."

Oliver Cromwell
(1599-1658), Lord
Protector of England[38]

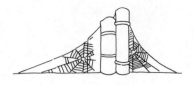

LEGAL LYRICS

The Law Is a Ass

Some say men on the back of the law
May ride and rule it like a patient ass
And with a golden bridle in the mouth
Direct it into anything they please.

Nathan Field (1587-c.1620), English lyricist [41]

CLIENTS, HEAL THYSELVES

The English poet and satirist Samuel Butler (1612-1680), is said to have lost a fortune due to the unskillfulness or embezzlement of a lawyer. But Butler's loss is posterity's gain: His expressions of loathing for the legal profession have become a part of the great edifice of English literature. Here are a couple of chunks:

A client is fain to hire a lawyer to keep from the injury
of other lawyers—as Christians in Turkey are forced to
hire Janissaries, to protect them from the insolences of
other Turks.[42]

And in his most famous work, *Hudibras*, he wrote:

So lawyers, lest the bear defendant,
And plaintiff dog, should make an end on't
Do stave and tail with writs of error,
Reverse of judgment, and demurrer,

To let them breathe a while, and then
Cry whoop, and set them on again.
Others believe no voice t'an organ
So sweet as lawyer's in his bar-gown,
Until, with subtle cobweb cheats,
They're catch'd in knotted law, like nets;
In which, when once they are imbrangled,
The more they stir, the more they're tangled;
And while their purses can dispute,
There's no end of th' immortal suit.

While lawyers have more sober sense
Than t'argue at their own expense,
But make their best advantages
Of others' quarrels, like the Swiss;
And out of foreign controversies,
By aiding both sides, fill their purses

"He who tries to fix and determine everything by law will inflame rather than correct the vices of the world."

Baruch Spinoza
(1632-1677),
Dutch philosopher[44]

He that with injury is griev'd,
And goes to law to be reliev'd,
Is sillier than a sottish chouse,
Who, when a thief has robb'd his house,
Applies himself to cunning men,
To help him to his goods again,
When all he can expect to gain,
Is but to squander more in vain.[43]

LEGAL LYRICS

Dispensing with Justice

Sir Samuel Garth (1661-1719), was an English poet and physician who was born at Yorkshire. His satirical poem "The Dispensary," published in 1699, was mainly aimed at his own profession and the still-familiar lament of the lack of medical services for the poor. But he saved some verses for lawyers:

Since of each enterprize th'Events unknown,
We'll quit the Sword and hearken to the Gown;
Nigh lives Vagellius, one reputed long,

For Strength of Lungs, and Pliancy of Tongues;
For Fees to any Form he moulds a Case,
The Worst has Merits, and the Best has Flaws.
Five Guinea's make a criminal to Day,
And then to Morrow wipe the Stain away;

To Law, then Friends, for 'tis by Fate decreed,
Vagellius and our Mony, shall succeed.[45]

NOTES

1 Irving Browne, *Law and Lawyers in Literature*, Soule and Bugbee, Boston, 1883 (reprinted by Wm. W. Gaunt & Sons, Inc., Holmes Beach, Florida, 1982) pg. 130.

2 Rosalind Ferguson, *The Penguin Dictionary of Proverbs*, Allen Lane, London, 1983, pg.138.

3 This definition of the Rule against Perpetuities is from Cheshire's *Modern Real Property*, quoted in René A. Wormser, *The Story of the Law*, Simon & Schuster, New York, 1962, pg. 272.

4 Erasmus, *The Praise of Folly* from *The Essential Erasmus*, New American Library, New York, 1964, pg. 142. Translated by John P. Dolan.

5 C.P. Curtis, *It's Your Law*, Harvard University Press, Cambridge, 1954, pg.33 and Martin Mayer, *The Lawyers*, Harper & Row, New York, 1967, pg. 230.

6 Browne, *Law and Lawyers in Literature*, pg.130.

7 Browne, *Law and Lawyers in Literature*, pgs. 203-4.

8 Robert Christy, *Proverbs, Maxims and Phrases*, G.P. Putnam's Sons, New York, 1907, pg. 600.

9 Rodney R. Jones, Charles M. Sevilla and Gerald F. Uelmen, *Disorderly Conduct*, W.W. Norton, New York, 1987, pg. 31.

10 C.W. Brooks, *Pettyfoggers and Vipers of the Commonwealth*, Cambridge University Press, London, 1986, pgs. 112-13.

11 Christopher Marlowe, *The Tragical History of the Life and Death of Doctor Faustus*, Act I, Scene 1, ll. 27-36.

12 W. Carew Hazlitt, *English Proverbs and Proverbial Phrases*, Reeves & Turner, London, 1907, pg. 425.

13 Tryon Edwards, *Useful Quotations*, Grosset & Dunlap, New York, 1936, pg. 326.

14 Wormser, *The Story of the Law*, pgs. 277-78; Thomas Coventry, *A Readable Edition of Coke upon Littleton*, London, 1830, pgs. xx, xxxvi.

15 Charles Warren, *A History of the American Bar*, Little, Brown and Co., Boston, 1911 (reprinted by William S. Hein, Buffalo, NY, 1980), pg. 22.

16 Bishop Hall, *Third Satire of the Second Book*, quoted in Browne, *Law and Lawyers in Literature*, pgs. 213-14.

17 C.W. Brooks, *Pettyfoggers and Vipers of the Commonwealth*, pg. 121; see B. Cozens-Hardy "Norfolk Lawyers," *Norfolk Archaeology*, 33 (1965) pgs. 266-79.

18 Charles Rembar, *The Law of the Land: The Evolution of Our Legal System*, Simon and Schuster, New York, 1980, pg. 299.

19 Robert Burton, *The Anatomy of Melancholy*, quoted in Simon James and Chantel Stebbings, *A Dictionary of Legal Quotations*, Macmillan, New York, 1987, pg. 121.

20 Wormser, *The Story of the Law*, pgs. 279-80.

21 J.A. Green, *The History of the English People*, Harper and Brothers, New York, 1878, pg. 592.

22 Wormser, *The Story of the Law*, pgs. 275-86.

23 Warren, *A History of the American Bar*, pg. 4.

24 Daniel Boorstin, *The Americans: The Colonial Experience*, 1958, pg. 197.

25 Warren, *A History of the American Bar*, pg. 105.

26 Ralph Warner, *Independent Paralegal's Handbook*, Nolo Press, Berkeley, 1987, pg. 8.

27 Warren, *A History of the American Bar*, pg. 41.

28 Warren, *A History of the American Bar*, pg. 121.

29 Wormser, *The Story of the Law*, pg. 317.

30 L.M. Friedman, *A History of American Law*, Simon & Schuster, New York, 1985, pg. 94.

31 Warren, *A History of the American Bar*, pgs. 67-8.

32 Warren, *A History of the American Bar*, pgs. 68-9.

33 Warren, *A History of the American Bar*, pg. 6.

34 Frank and Fritzie Manuel, *Utopian Thought in the Western World*, Belknap/Harvard University Press, Cambridge, 1979, pg. 337.

35 Don M. Wolfe, *Leveller Manifestoes of the Puritan Revolution*, Humanities Press, New York, 1967, pg. 192.

36 *The New Law of Righteousness*, 1649, quoted in Louise M. Berneri, *Journey through Utopia*, London, 1950, pg. 161.

37 Wilfred R. Prest, (ed.), *Lawyers in Early Modern Europe and America*, Holmes & Meier Publishers, New York, 1981, pg. 76.

38 Prest, (ed.), *Lawyers in Early Modern Europe and America*, pg. 76.

39 Warren, *A History of the American Bar*, pgs. 6-7, 10-11.

40 Christy, *Proverbs*, pg. 608.

41 Nathan Field, *Woman is a Weathercock* (1609), Act II, from H.L. Mencken, *A New Dictionary of Quotations on Historical Principles*, Alfred E. Knopf, New York, 1942, pg. 656.

42 Samuel Butler, *Prose Observations*, 1660-80, from John Gross (ed.), *Oxford Book of Aphorisms*, Oxford University Press, Oxford, 1983, pg. 111.

43   Samuel Butler, *Hudibras*, 1663, quoted in Browne, *Law and Lawyers in Literature*, pgs. 223-25.

44   Mayer, *The Lawyers*, pg. 119.

45   Samuel Garth, *The Dispensary*, Canto IV, ll. 156-163 in *Garth's "Dispensary,"* Wilhelm J. Leicht (ed.), Carl Winter, Heidelberg, 1905, pg. 83.

CHAPTER FOUR

THE
EIGHTEENTH
CENTURY

HISTORICAL BRIEF

Storms of Forms

Never a model of efficiency, by the Eighteenth Century, the English legal system had become ossified and perverse. Form had completely overrun content. Before any legal action began, there was an elaborate and unbending ritual called "special pleading." This consisted of each side presenting specific pre-fab forms and then in turn attesting to a certain argument or defense.

These forms, established in the Middle Ages, had names like *nul disseisin, nihil debet, non assumpsit* and similar Latinisms that the uninitiated, including clients, were certain not to understand. The plaintiff (the plaintiff's well-remunerated lawyer, really) had to file just the right form of plea out of the hundreds available; the defendant had to answer with precisely the correct reply. The plaintiff answered with another form. Again, it had to be the correct one, or the case would be thrown out. The defendant then replied to this, again careful to choose the correct form, lest the case be lost immediately. This went back and forth, through thickets of bastardized and archaic French and Latin, and all before any kind of trial or even oral arguments could begin.[1]

Litigants lost in this paperstorm of Declarations, Avoidances, Pleas in Confessions, Replications, Rejoinders, Surrejoinders, Rebutters and Surrebutters could seek shelter only in the arms of a lawyer, the very character who raised the wind in the first place. As an article published in *Punch* in 1899 put it:

> *In every subject of dispute with two sides to it, there is a right and a wrong; but in the style of putting the contending statements so as to confuse the right and the wrong together, the science of special pleading consists. This system is of such remote antiquity that nobody knows the beginning of it, and this accounts for no one being able to appreciate its end. The accumulated chicanery and blundering of several generations, called in forensic language the wisdom of successive ages, gradually brought special pleading into its present shape, or, rather, into its present endless forms. Its extensive drain on the pockets of the suitors has rendered it always an important branch of legal study; while, when properly understood, it appears an instrument so beautifully calculated for distributive justice, that, when brought to bear upon property, it will often distribute the whole of it among the lawyers and leave nothing for the litigants themselves.[2]*

HARD TIMES FOR CRIMES

While many people consider the Eighteenth Century to be the Age of Reason, in many respects British legal procedure had not changed since the Middle Ages. Those accused of crimes were confined along with convicts in primitive, filthy cells and compounds. Everyone was thrown together regardless of age, sex or charge. The jailors rarely fed the inmates, and the accused who had no money or relatives willing to bring them food were liable to starve. Various methods of torture were still used both to obtain confessions and to punish. The number of capital offenses had grown from about fifty in 1688 to over 160 in 1765. The death penalty was imposed, for example, for stealing five shillings, for fortune-telling and for destroying a fishpond.[3]

THE DELAY OF THE LAW

It's the Pits

John Arbuthnot (1667-1735), the Scottish scientist, physician and author, was a friend of Jonathan Swift, with whom he shared both a penchant for satire and an intense loathing of lawyers. Arbuthnot's *History of John Bull* was a political parody, but he could not resist firing a few barbed arrows at the legal tribe:

> Law is a bottomless pit, it is a cormorant, a harpy, that devours everything. John Bull [the plaintiff] was flattered by his lawyers that his suit would not last above a year or two at most; that before that time he would be in quiet possession of his business. Yet ten long years did Hocus [the lawyer] steer his cause through all the meanders of the law and all the courts. No skills, no address, was wanting; and to say truth, John did not starve the cause; there wanted not yellow-boys to fee counsel, hire witnesses, and bribe juries. Lord Strutt [the defendant] was generally cast, never had one verdict in his favour; and John was promised that the next would be the final determination; but alas! that final determination and happy conclusion was like an enchanted island, the nearer John came to it the further it went from him. New trials upon new points still arose; new doubts, new matters to be cleared; in short, lawyers seldom part with so good a cause till they have got the oyster and their clients the shell. John's ready money, boot-debts, bonds, mortgages, all went into the lawyer's pockets. Then John began to borrow money upon bank stock and East India bonds; now and then a farm went to pot.[4]

LEGAL LYRICS

Defining De Foe

English author Daniel Defoe (1660-1731), was in court a number of times for debts and for political pamphleteering, and no doubt got his fill of English justice after standing in the pillory on three separate occasions. This stanza is from "A Hymn To The Pillory:"

> Next bring some lawyers to thy bar,
> By innuendo they might all stand there;
> There let them expiate their guilt,
> And pay for all that blood their tongues ha'spilt,
> These are the mountebanks of state.
> Who by the slight of tongue can crimes create,
> And dress up trifles in the robes of fates.[5]

THE LACK OF COMMON SENSE IN THE COMMON LAW

Under the English common law in the Eighteenth Century, a defendant in a felony trial—and a felony involved any theft over five pounds—had no right to counsel in court. However, if the defendant could find an error in the phrasing of the indictment, counsel would be provided—not to defend the prisoner, but to quibble over the legitimacy of the bill of indictment. The English lawyer John W. Smith versified this absurd, chilling logic:

> The speedy arm of Justice was never known to fail;
> The gaol supplied the gallows, the gallows thinned the gaol,
> And sundry wise precautions the sages of the law,
> Discreetly framed whereby they aimed to keep the rogues in awe.
> For lest some sturdy criminal false witnesses should bring,
> His witnesses were not allowed to swear to anything.
> And lest his wily advocate the court should overreach,
> His advocate was not allowed the privilege of speech.
> Yet such was the humanity and wisdom of the law,
> That if in his indictment there appeared to be a flaw,
> The court assigned him counsellors to argue on the doubt.
> Provided he himself had first contrived to point it out.
> Yet lest their mildness should, perchance, be craftily abused,
> To show him the indictment they most sturdily refused.
> But still, that he might understand the nature of the charge,
> The same was in the Latin tongue read out to him at large.
> 'Twas thus the law kept rogues at awe, gave honest men protection,
> And justly framed, by all was named, of widsom the perfection.[7]

BETTER LATE THAN NEVER

In 1733, Parliament finally prevailed on the courts to use the English language in special pleadings and proceedings. Recall that the first statute to direct that English be used in English courts had been promulgated 371 years earlier. Latin and law French phrases continue to clog legal discourse to this day.[8]

AN UNLEARNED CLASS

The Eighteenth Century English law student was hardly a student at all—legal education was nearly nonexistent. The mootings, readings and exercises that made up a law education at the Inns of Court in the previous century had almost completely died out. There were no classes to attend and no required readings. A student could (and doubtless many did) graduate without having broken the spine of a book or reading a single page of law. The future lawyers of the nation were notorious for all-night jags in taverns and revels in the cheap pleasures of London. *The Spectator* of March 24, 1710, complained of "those young men who being placed in the Inns of Court in order to study the laws of their country frequent the playhouse more than Westminster Hall and are seen in all public assemblies except in a court of justice."[9]

All that was required of the law student to become a counselor-at-law was proof that all fees were paid and that the prescribed number of dinners had been eaten in the Inn. They were then free to hang out shingles and bill an unsuspecting public as heartily as they wished.[10]

"Law, like orthodoxy in religion, is a mystery where reason ends and faith begins; none of the uninitiated can enter even the vestibule of the temple; society knows nothing about it but by means of the lawyer."

Anthony Ashley Cooper, 3rd Earl of Shaftesbury (1671-1713)[6]

LEGAL LYRICS

Better a Buccaneer than a Barrister Be

Meanwhile, back in America, the Colonists were still reeling from their first bad experience with lawyers, who were still held in the highest disregard. Dan C. Rule, Jr. wrote the following verse set in Colonial Massachussets. Entitled *Ye Fallen Pirate*, it treats the conversion of an early lawyer from his wicked ways:

One Time there dwelt in Boston Towne—
'Twas during bluff King George's Reign—
An Advocate of wide Renowne
Ycleped Ezekiel Reuben Kayne,

Who on ye Lidde so firmly sat
Of his past Life & Historie,

That folk referred to him as "That
Strange, silent Man of Mysterie."

He hearkened not unto ye Chimes
That call to Prayer on Sabbath Day,
But sought ye Tavern, & for Dimes
At Seven-Uppe with Cardes would play.

But our good Parson, Matthew Birch,
One Nighte sought out ye Lawyer Kayne:
"Why comes our Brother not to Church?
Speak up, my erring Son—explain!"

Then Lawyer Kayne he bowed his Hedde
& wept right betterlie & sore.
"Tis little use," he sobbing said,
"For I be lost forever more!

A Lawyer now; but in my Youth
(At last I speak out bold & plain),
I was (good Parson, hear the truth!)
A Pirate on ye Spanish Main!"

Our Parson sighed. "Why not retrace
Ye path by which ye fell so low?
By far ye swiftest Road to Grace
Is that by which we travel slow.

One upward Step is plain to see,
For what ye lost ye must regain;
Go back, O Lawyer Kayne, & be
A pirate on ye Spanish Main!"[11]

SELECTIONS FROM A MASTER

Jonathan Swift (1667-1745)

Swift, one of the great satirists in the English language, was born in Dublin. While his verses lambasted all the various hypocrisies of his day, he saved many of his sharpest barbs for lawyers:

On Dreams

In this poem, Swift satirized the nightly visions of various professions, including the lawyers:

Orphans around his bed the lawyer sees.
And takes the plaintiff's and defendant's fees,
His fellow pick-purse, watching for a job,
Fancies his fingers in the cully's fob.[12]

Gulliver's Travels

In Part II of Swift's most famous work, Lemuel Gulliver is stranded in Brobdingnag, the land of Giants. In a conversation with the King, he describes the justice system in his native England, but meets with a certain skepticism:

> *I then descended to the Courts of Justice, over which the Judges, those venerable Sages and Interpreters of the Law, presided, for determining the disputed Rights and Properties of Men, as well as for the Punishment of Vice, and Protection of Innocence . . . .*

> *Upon what I said in relation to our Courts of Justice, his Majesty desired to be satisfied in several points: and this I was the better able to do, having been formerly almost ruined by a long Suit in Chancery, which was decreed for me with Costs. He asked what Time was usually spent in determining between Right and Wrong, and what Degree of Expence. Whether Advocates and Orators had Liberty to plead in causes manifestly known to be unjust, vexatious, or oppressive. Whether Party in Religion or Politics were observed to be of any Weight in the Scale of Justice. Whether those pleading orators were persons educated in the general Knowledge of Equity, or only in provincial, national or other local Customs. Whether they or their judges had any Part in penning those Laws which they assumed the Liberty of inter- preting and glossing upon at their Pleasure. Whether they had ever at different Times pleaded for and against the same Cause, and cited Precedents to prove contrary opinions. Whether they were a rich or a poor Corpora- tion. Whether they received any pecuniary Reward for pleading or delivering their opinions. And particularly whether they were ever admitted as Members in the lower Senate. . . .*

> *His Majesty . . . taking me into his Hands, and stroaking me gently, delivered himself in these Words, which I shall never forget or the manner he spoke them in. "My little friend . . . you have made a most admirable Panegyrick upon your Country. You have clearly proved . . . that Laws are best explained, interpreted, and applied by those whose Interests and Abilities lie in perverting, confounding, and eluding them."*[13]

Later, Gulliver travels to the land of the noble and intelligent horses called Houyhnhnms. One of the Houyhnhnms questions Gulliver as to the strange customs of his native land:

I had said that some of our Crew left their Country on Account of being ruined by Law: that I had already explained the meaning of the word: but he was at a Loss how it should come to pass, that the Law which was intended for every Man's Preservation, should be any Man's Ruin. Therefore he desired to be further satisfied what I meant by Law, and the dispensers thereof, according to the present Practice in my own Country: because he thought Nature and Reason were sufficient Guides for a reasonable animal, as we pretended to be, in shewing us what we ought to do, and what to avoid.

I assured his Honour that Law was a Science wherein I had not much conversed, further than by employing Advocates, in vain, upon some Injustices that had been done me. However, I would give him all the Satisfaction I was able.

I said there was a Society of men among us, bred up from their youth in the art of proving by Words multiplied for the Purpose, that White is Black, and Black is White, according as they are paid. To this Society all the rest of the People are Slaves.

For Example. If my Neighbour hath a mind to my Cow, he hires a Lawyer to prove that he ought to have my Cow from me. I must then hire another to defend my Right: it being against all Rules of Law that any man should be allowed to speak for himself. Now in this case, I who am the true Owner lie under two great Disadvantages. First my Lawyer being practiced almost from his Cradle in defending falshood is quite out of his element when he would be an Advocate for Justice, which as an Office unnatural, he always attempts with great Awkwardness, if not with Ill-will. The second Disadvantage is that my lawyer must proceed with great caution: Or else he will be reprimanded by the judges, and abhorred by his Brethren, as one who would lessen the Practice of the Law. And therefore I have but two Methods to preserve my Cow. The first is to gain over my Adversary's Lawyer with a double Fee; who will then betray his Client, by insinuating that he hath Justice on his Side. The second way is for my Lawyer to make my Cause appear as unjust as he can; by allowing the Cow to belong to my Adversary; and this if it be skillfully done, will certainly bespeak the favour of the Bench.

Now, your Honour is to know, that these Judges are Persons appointed to decide all Controversies of Property, as well as for the Tryal of Criminals; and picked out from the most dextrous Lawyers who are grown old or lazy; and having been byassed all their Lives against Truth and Equity, are under such a fatal Necessity of favoring Fraud, Perjury, and Oppression, that I have known some of them to have refused a large Bribe from the side where justice lay, rather than injure the Faculty, by doing anything unbecoming their nature or their office.

It is a Maxim among these Lawyers, that whatever hath been done before may legally be done again: And therefore they take special Care to record all the Decisions formerly made against the common justice and the general Reason of mankind. These, under the name of Precedents, they produce as Authorities to justify the most iniquitous Opinions; and the Judges never fail of decreeing accordingly.

In pleading, they studiously avoid entering into the Merits of the Cause; but are loud, violent, and tedious in dwelling upon all circumstances which are not to the Purpose. For Instance, in the Case already mentioned, they never desire to know what Claim or Title my Adversary hath to my Cow; but whether said Cow were Red or Black; her Horns long or short; whether the Field I graze her upon be round or square; whether she were milked at home or abroad; what Diseases she is subject to, and the like. After which they consult Precedents, adjourn the Cause, from Time to Time, and in Ten, Twenty, or Thirty years come to an Issue.

It is likewise to be observed, that this Society hath a peculiar Cant or Jargon of their own, that no other Mortal can understand, and wherein all their Laws are written, which they take special Care to multiply; whereby they have wholly confounded the very Essence of Truth and Falsehood, of Right and Wrong; so that it will take Thirty Years to decide whether the Field, left me by my Ancestors for six Generations, belong to me, or to a Stranger three Hundred Miles off.

In the tryal of Persons accused for Crimes against the State, the Method is much more short and commendable: the Judge first sends to sound the disposition of those in Power; after which he can easily hang or save the Criminal, strictly preserving all the forms of Law.

Here my master interposing said it was a Pity that creatures endowed with such prodigious Abilities of Mind as these Lawyers, by the description I have of them must certainly be, were not rather encouraged to be Instructors of others in Wisdom and Knowledge. In Answer to which, I assured his Honour that in all Points out of their own Trade, they were usually the most ignorant and stupid Generation among us, the most despicable in common conversation, avowed enemies to all knowledge and learning; and equally disposed to pervert the general Reason of Mankind, in every other Subject of Discourse as in that of their own Profession.[14]

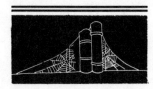

GAY'S DREARY ASSESSMENT

A contemporary of Swift's was poet and playwright John Gay (1685-1732). In 1727, he published a popular collection of fables, one of which, "The Dog and the Fox," is addressed to a lawyer and is introduced as follows:

I know you lawyers can with ease,
Twist words and meanings as you please;
That language, by your skill made pliant,
Will bend to favor every client;
That 'tis the fee directs the sense,
To make out either side's pretense.
When you peruse the clearest case,
You see it with a double face;
For scepticism is your profession:
You hold there's doubt in all expression.

Hence is the bar with fees supplied,
Hence eloquence takes either side.
Your hand would have but paltry gleaning,
Could every man express his meaning.
Who dares presume to pen a deed,
Unless you previously are fee'd?
'Tis drawn, and to augment the cost,
In dull prolixity engrost;
And now we're well secured by law,
Till the next brother find a flaw.

Read o'er a will. Was't ever known
But you could make the will your own?
For when you read, 'tis with intent
To find out meanings never meant.
Since things are thus, se defendendo,
I bar fallacious innuendo.[15]

AN ENLIGHTENED VIEW

The great French philosopher and writer Voltaire (1694-1778), was also fervently unenthusiastic about lawyers and laws:

I was never ruined but twice—once when I lost a lawsuit, and once when I gained one.[17]

and

A multitude of laws in a country is . . . a sign of weakness and malady.[18]

and

The worthy administrators of justice are like a cat set to take care of a cheese, lest it should be gnawed by the mice. One bite of the cat does more damage than twenty mice can do.[19]

POOR RICHARD'S LAWSUIT

The great American wit Benjamin Franklin (1706-1790), dispensed a lot of homespun wisdom about lawyers. For example: "Necessity knows no law, I know some attorneys of the same."[20] And "God works wonders now and then; Behold! a lawyer, an honest man."[21]

In a poem entitled "The Benefit of Going to Law," published in *Poor Richard's Almanack* in 1733, he warns the potential litigant:

Two Beggars travelling along,
One blind, the other lame
Picked up an Oyster on the way,
To which they both laid claim:
The matter rose so high, that they
Resolved to go to Law,
As often richer Fools have done,
Who quarrel for a Straw.
A Lawyer took it straight in hand,
Who knew his business was
To mind nor one nor t'other side,
But make the best o'th' Cause.
As always in the Law's the Case,
So he his Judgement gave,
And Lawyer like he thus resolve'd
What each of them should have.
Blind Plaintif, lame Defendant share,
The friendly Law's impartial Care:
A Shell for him, a Shell for thee;
The MIDDLE is the Lawyer's Fee.[22]

> **"Sometimes a man who deserves to be looked down upon because he is a fool is despised only because he is a lawyer."**
>
> Charles de Secondat (1689-1755), Baron de Montesquieu[16]

UNDERGROUND HUMOR

Lord Norbury, known as The Hanging Judge, was famous for his wit, although it was probably not appreciated by defendants. Here is a sample of his less lethal humor:

When asked to contribute a shilling to bury a poor attorney, Lord Norbury replied: "Only a shilling to bury an attorney? Here's a guinea, go and bury one and twenty of them."[23]

> *"I do not care to speak ill of a man behind his back, but I believe the gentleman is an attorney."*
>
> Samuel Johnson (1709-1784), English lexicographer[24]

THE HIGH COST OF JUSTICE

No matter what the era, price fixing has often occurred when two or more lawyers get together. Legal scholar Lawrence M. Friedman describes this practice among Colonial lawyers in his *History of American Law:*

> *In Rhode Island, eight lawyers signed a "Compact" in 1745 to make sure fees would always be "sufficient for our support and subsistence." No case was to be pleaded at Superior Court for less than a three pound fee; only a "standing client" was "to be trusted without his note." Attorneys were not to sign "blank writs and disperse them about the colony, which practice . . . would make the law cheap." They agreed not to defend any client whose lawyer was suing for his fee unless three or more "brethren" determined that the lawyer's demand was "unreasonable."* [25]

PRESIDENTIAL WISDOM

The Second President on the Second Oldest Profession

> *Let us look upon a lawyer. In the beginning of life we see him fumbling and raking amidst the rubbish of writs, indictments, pleas, ejectments, enfiefed, illatebration and one thousand other* lignum vitae *words which have neither harmony nor meaning. When he gets into business, he often foments more quarrels than he composes, and enrichs himself at the expense of impoverishing others more honest and deserving than himself.*
>
> John Adams (1735-1826)[26]

THE LABYRINTH OF LEGAL LANGUAGE

The poet, Samuel Bishop, on legal language:

In indenture or deed
Tho' a thousand you read
Neither comma nor colon you'll ken;
A stop intervening,
Might determine the meaning
And what would the lawyers do then? [28]

"One lawsuit
breeds twenty."

Scottish Proverb[27]

ROGUES GALLERY

William Blackstone (1723-1780)

William Blackstone is considered a towering figure in legal thought. His *Commentaries on the Laws of England* are well known and were required reading for law students for at least a century. Indeed, it was not until recently that Blackstone's reputation as the wisest of lawyers has come into question.

Born at Cheapside in 1723, Blackstone went to Oxford and then entered the Middle Temple of London's Inns of Court in 1741. Five years later, he started a law practice. He failed. In 1753, he tried to get a professorship in Roman Law at Oxford through the influence of Lord Mansfield. He failed. He then began reading private law lectures at Oxford. It was his first success: His lectures proved so popular that a chair in English law, the first at Oxford, was endowed for him.

The quality of these lectures, though, is questionable. As legal scholar and Blackstone biographer Vernon X. Miller put it: "He had only the vaguest possible grasp of the elementary conceptions of the law. He evidently regarded the law of gravitation, the law of nature and the law of England as different examples of one principle—as rules of action or conduct imposed by a superior power on its subjects . . . . Whether through the natural conservatism of a lawyer, or through his own timidity and subserviency as a man and politician, he is always found to be a specious defender of the existing order of things."[29] And Jeremy Bentham, the English Utilitarian, who attended Blackstone's lectures at the tender age of sixteen, later declared that the professor was a "formal, precise and affected lecturer—just what you would expect from the character of his writings—cold, reserved and wary, exhibiting a frigid pride."[30]

Blackstone's subserviency paid off for him for the rest of his life. In 1761, he was made a King's Counsel, and shortly thereafter was elected to Parliament, "because," explains historian

René Wormser, "he was corruptible, and his record shows that he always willing to do the bidding of his principals, who were of the government party."[31] The pseudonymous "Junius," a still-unidentified correspondent of the day, reveals the contemporary reputation of Doctor Blackstone: "For the defence of truth, of law, and reason, the Doctor's book may be safely consulted; but whoever wishes to cheat a neighbour of his estate, or to rob a country of its rights, need make no scruple of consulting the Doctor himself."[32]

In a legal dispute over the seating of a political enemy in Parliament, Blackstone truculently supported the Crown, asserting that the member, who had once been expelled from Parliament, had no right to ever be reelected. He insisted the common law backed him up until an opponent read aloud in Parliament a section from the *Commentaries* on the subject that made no mention of prior expulsion. Blackstone was silenced—at least until the second edition of the *Commentaries*, when, lo and behold, his position suddenly appeared as part of the hoary and venerated common law of England.

Blackstone proved so pliant that he was knighted and promoted by King George III to a judgeship in 1770. His career on the bench was characterized by an almost total lack of distinction, and although his *Commentaries* are often cited, particularly in American case law, his own decisions as a judge never are. On the bench his toadyism grew boundless to the point of absurdity. He once said: "That the king can do no wrong is a necessary and fundamental principle of the English constitution." On later reflection, considering that sentiment too liberal, he stated: "The king is not only incapable of doing wrong, but even of thinking wrong: in him there is no folly or weakness." This stunning bit of nonsense, it should be noted, was uttered during the reign of the insane George III.

Blackstone was a corpulent and sedentary man, and was never in good health. It was said that the gout and nervous disorders that he suffered from were the cause of the exceeding peevishness he displayed in court, but then again, it might just have been his natural disposition. In the winter of 1779, he contracted a case of dropsy, and after a short illness, died on February 14, 1780 at the age of 57.

BURKE BITES

Edmund Burke (1729-1797), is of course known for his brilliant career in politics and letters, but he first came to London in 1750 to study law at the Middle Temple. Fortunately, he was never licensed to practice, and the world gained a philosopher.

Based, presumably, on first-hand experience, he left these reflections on the legal profession:

> *A good parson once said, that where mystery begins,*
> *religion ends. Cannot I say, as truly at last, of human*
> *laws, that where mystery begins justice ends? It is hard*
> *to see whether the doctors of law or divinity have made*
> *the greater advances in the lucrative business of*
> *mystery.*[33]

ESQ., R.I.P.

The following epitaph, written by Oliver Goldsmith (1728-1774), recalls the sentiment of the day on attorneys:

> *Here Hickey reclines, a most blunt, pleasant creature;*
> *And slander itself must allow him good nature:*
> *He cherish'd his friend, and he relish'd a bumper;*
> *Yet one fault he had, and that one was a thumper.*
> *Perhaps you may ask if the man was a miser?*
> *I answer, No, no, for he always was wiser.*
> *Too courteous, perhaps, or obligingly flat?*
> *His very worst foe can't accuse him of that.*
> *Perhaps he confided in men as they go,*
> *And so was too foolishly honest? Ah, no!*
> *Then, what was his failing? come, tell it, and burn ye:*
> *He was—could he help it? a special attorney.*[34]

THE WEALTH OF LAWYERS

Adam Smith (1723-1790), did not think that lawyers were a productive part of the capitalist economy. In fact, he classed lawyers with "the most frivolous professions" such as "players, buffoons, musicians and opera-singers" as economically useless. In *The Wealth of Nations*, he wrote:

> *It has been the custom in modern Europe to regulate,*
> *upon most occasions, the payments of the attorneys and*
> *clerks of courts according to the number of pages which*
> *they had occasion to write; the court, however, requir-*
> *ing, that each page should contain so many lines, and*
> *each line so many words. In order to increase their*
> *payment, the attorneys and clerks have contrived to*
> *multiply words beyond all necessity, to the corruption of*
> *the law language of, I believe, every court of justice in*
> *Europe.*[35]

A DECLARATION OF INDEPENDENCE

On July 25, 1776, just three weeks after the Declaration of Independence was adopted, Timothy Dwight (1752-1817), a Yale professor of divinity, and later president of the college, warned the graduating class of the evils of the legal profession in no uncertain terms:

> *That meaness, that infernal knavery, which multiplies needless litigations, which retards the operation of justice, which, from court to court, upon the most trifling pretences, postpones trial to glean the last emptyings of a client's pocket, for unjust fees of everlasting attendance, which artfully twists the meaning of law to the side we espouse, which seizes unwarrantable advantages from the prepossessions, ignorance, interests and prejudices of a jury, you will shun rather than death or infamy.*[36]

THOSE WERE THE GOOD OLD DAYS

The historian J. B. McMaster wrote that during the early American Republic:

"... [lawyers] were denounced as banditti, as bloodsuckers, as pickpockets, as windbags, as smooth-tongued rogues .... The mere sight of a lawyer ... was enough to call forth an oath or a muttered curse . . . ."[37]

SOME JEFFERSONISMS

The great American statesman Thomas Jefferson (1743-1826), himself a lawyer, had an intimate familiarity with the effect of the legal profession on society:

> *Knowing that religion does not furnish greater bigots than law, I expect little from old judges.*[38]

And, referring to the U.S. Congress:

> *That one hundred and fifty lawyers should do business together ought not to be expected.*[39]

Jefferson also remarked:

> *It is the trade of lawyers to question everything and talk by the hour.*[40]

A MODEST PROPOSAL

Soon after the Revolution, the Massachusetts town of Dedham, suffering under the tireless work of lawyers in collecting debts, representing Tories and English citizens in recovering property and throwing patriots in prison for debt, instructed its representatives to send the following message to the State Legislature:

> *We are not inattentive to the almost universally prevailing complaints against the practice of the order of lawyers; and many of us now sensibly feel the effects of their unreasonable and extravagant exactions; we think their practice pernicious and their mode unconstitutional. You will therefore endeavor that such regulations be introduced into our Courts of Law, and that such restraints be laid on the order of lawyers as that we may have recourse to the Laws and find our security and not our ruin in them. If upon a fair discussion and mature deliberation such a measure should appear impracticable, you are to endeavor that the order of Lawyers be totally abolished; an alternative preferable to their continuing in their present mode.[41]*

THE LABYRINTH OF LEGAL LANGUAGE

Bigger, But No Better

> *It will be of little avail to the people that the laws are made by men of their own choice if the laws be so voluminous that they cannot be read, or so incoherent that they cannot be understood; if they be repealed or revised before they are promulgated, or undergo such incessant changes that no man, who knows what the law is today can guess what it will be tomorrow.*

Alexander Hamilton (1757-1804), American statesman[42]

THE BOTANY OF THE BAR

J. Hector St. John Crevecoeur (1735-1813), was born in France, but in 1769 bought a farm in Orange, New York. An author and agriculturist (he introduced alfalfa into the United States), he wrote *Letters from an American Farmer* in 1782:

> *Lawyers are plants that will grow in any soil that is cultivated by the hands of others; and when once they have taken root they will extinguish every other vegetable that grows around them. The fortunes they daily acquire in every province, from the misfortunes of their fellow citizens, are surprising. The most ignorant, the*

most bungling member of that profession will, if placed in the most obscure part of the country, promote litigiousness and amass more wealth than the most opulent farmer with all his toil . . . . What a pity that our forefathers who happily extinguished so many fatal customs and expunged from their new government so many errors and abuses both religious and civil, did not also prevent the introduction of a set of men so dangerous . . . . They are here what the clergy were in past centuries . . . . A reformation equally useful is now wanted.[43]

AMERICAN FREEDOM A SETBACK FOR LAWYERS

The American Revolution, which introduced an era of previously unknown freedom for the common person, was the beginning of a period of decline for the legal profession. This is partly because most of the lawyers sided with the King rather than the Continental Congress. Thomas Jefferson wrote to James Madison: "Our lawyers are all Tories." Many lawyers left for England or Canada after Yorktown. There are no reports of sorrow at this exodus.

Another reason for the decline was that Americans viewed the English legal system, with its formal rules and emphasis of technical procedure, as fundamentally undemocratic. They were right. There was tremendous opposition to the adoption of English law, and particularly an English-style bar in America.

Many people felt that individuals should represent themselves in their legal disputes. A self-help law book entitled *Every Man His Own Lawyer* was a bestseller in the young United States, going into a ninth edition by 1784.[44]

AN HONEST VIEW

Writing under the name of "Honestus," Benjamin Austin (1752-1820), an Anti-Federalist politician and pamphleteer of Boston, wrote *Observations on the Pernicious Practice of the Law* in 1786 to attack "the order of lawyers." He advised rather stringent measures:

The order is becoming continually more and more powerful . . . There is danger of lawyers becoming powerful as a combined body. The people should be guarded against it as it may subvert every principle of law and establish a perfect aristocracy . . . This order should be annihilated.[45]

We're Mad as Hell and We're Not Going to Take It Anymore . . .

Shays' Rebellion, an uprising of debtors and tenant farmers in western Massachusetts in 1786 and1787, was directed largely against the courts and lawyers. A band of some 800 insurgents, led by farmer Daniel Shays (c. 1747-1825), prevented the Court of Common Pleas from meeting and handing down decisions unfavorable to debtors. They finally allowed the court to sit only after it agreed not to convict farmers unable to pay their mortgages. The extent of anti-lawyer sentiment at the time is indicated by the fact that Shays' men then took up arms against the government and attacked an arsenal at Springfield. They were quickly routed. Shays was captured and condemned to death, but in what was probably the only judicial decision he was ever truly thankful for, he was pardoned.[47]

Liberté, Egalité, Fraternité and No Lawyers

By a decree of the French revolutionary National Assembly on September 2, 1790, French lawyers were outlawed. The ancient robes and musty wigs were discontinued, the term *avocat* was dropped, and the organized bar disbanded. Counsels—called *defenseurs officieux*—were still allowed in the courts, but without the requirement of admittance to the bar or a prescribed course of study. This unregulated state of affairs, however, was short-lived. In 1804, the Emperor Napoleon reestablished the bar with all its former pomp and pomposity.

NOTES

1   Charles Rembar, *The Law of the Land: The Evolution of Our Legal System,* Simon & Schuster, New York, 1980, pgs. 224-27.

2   Marshall Brown, *Wit and Humor of the Bench and Bar,* T.H. Flood & Co., Chicago, 1899 (reprinted by Fred B. Rothman & Co., Littleton, Colorado, 1986), pgs. 404-5.

3   Stephen Tumim, *Great Legal Fiascos,* Arthur Barker Ltd., London, 1985, pg. 41; René A. Wormser, *The Story of the Law,* Simon & Schuster, New York, 1962, pg. 218.

4   John Arbuthnot, *The History of John Bull,* Chapter 6, from George Aitken (ed.), *The Life and Works of John Arbuthnot,* Clarendon Press, Oxford, 1892, pgs. 204-5.

5   Daniel Defoe, *A Hymn to the Pillory,* (1703), quoted in Simon James and Chantel Stebbings, *A Dictionary of Legal Quotations,* Macmillan, New York, 1987, pg. 103.

6   Edward P. Day, *Day's Collacon: An Encyclopedia of Prose Quotations,* International, New York, 1884, pg. 496.

7   Brown, *Wit and Humor of the Bench and Bar,* pg. 281.

8   Charles Warren, *A History of the American Bar,* Little, Brown and Co., Boston, 1911 (reprinted by William S. Hein, Buffalo, NY, 1980), pg. 149.

9   Warren, *A History of the American Bar,* pg. 152.

10 Warren, *A History of the American Bar,* pgs. 151-6.

11 William L. Prosser, *The Judicial Humorist,* Little, Brown and Co., Boston, 1952, pgs. 6-7.

12 Jonathan Swift, *On Dreams* (1724) in Pat Rogers (ed.), *Jonathan Swift: The Complete Poems,* Penguin Books, New York, 1983, pg. 270.

13 Swift, *Gulliver's Travels,* Part II, Chapter 6 from Paul Turner (ed.), Swift: *Gulliver's Travels,* Oxford University Press, Oxford, 1971, pgs. 123-26.

14 Swift, *Gulliver's Travels,* Part IV, Chapter 5 from Turner, Swift, pgs. 251-54.

15 John Gay, "The Dog and the Fox" quoted in Irving Browne, *Law and Lawyers in Literature,* Soule and Bugbee, Boston, 1883 (reprinted by Wm. W. Gaunt & Sons, Inc., Holmes Beach, Florida, 1982), pgs. 238-39.

16 Baron de Montesquieu, Persian Letters, Letter 44 from *Chinese and Persian Letters,* M. Walter Dunne, Washington, DC, 1901, pg. 94. Translated by John Davidson.

17   Tryon Edwards, *Useful Quotations*, Grosset & Dunlop, New York, 1936, pg. 324.

18   Edwards, *Useful Quotations*, pg. 328.

19   Rhoda T. Tripp (ed.), *International Thesaurus of Quotations*, Thomas Y. Crowell, New York, 1970, pg. 331. Translated by Elizabeth Wykoff.

20   Benjamin Franklin, *Poor Richard's Almanack*, 1733, pg. 20 from *Poor Richard's Almanack, Being the Almanacks of 1733, 1749, 1756, 1757, 1758*, Doubleday, Doran & Co., Garden City (NJ), 1928, pgs. 9-10.

21   Tripp (ed.), *International Thesaurus of Quotations*, pg. 344.

22   Benjamin Franklin, *Poor Richard's Almanack*, 1733, pg. 20 from *Poor Richard's Almanack, Being the Almanacks of 1733, 1749, 1756, 1757, 1758*, pgs. 9-10.

23   Brown, *Wit and Humor of Bench and Bar*, pg. 364.

24   Mrs. Hester Piozzi, *Anecdotes of Johnson*, (1786), pg. 327 note, quoted in H.L. Mencken, *A New Dictionary of Quotations on Historical Principles*, Alfred A. Knopf, New York, 1942, pg. 666.

25   L.M. Friedman, *A History of American Law*, Simon & Schuster, New York, 1985, pgs. 100-1.

26   In the Nantucket Gazette (1817) quoted in Warren, *History of the American Bar*, pg. 79.

27   Selwyn Gurney Champion, *Racial Proverbs*, Barnes & Noble, New York, 1950, pg. 72.

28   Samuel Bishop, *Poems on Various Subjects*, Cadell & Davies, London, 1802, Vol. 2, pg. 161.

29   V.X. Miller, "William Blackstone," *Encyclopedia Britannica*, 14th Edition (1973) Vol. 3, pg. 749.

30   David A. Lockmiller, *Sir William Blackstone*, The University of North Carolina Press, Chapel Hill, 1938, pg. 50.

31   Wormser, *The Story of the Law*, pgs. 293-95.

32   Lockmiller, *Sir William Blackstone*, pg. 100.

33   Edmund Burke, *A Vindication of Natural Society*, quoted in Simon James and Chantal Stebbings, *A Dictionary of Legal Quotations*, Macmillan, New York, 1987, pgs. 16-17.

34   Browne, *Law and Lawyers in Literature*, pg. 250.

35   Adam Smith, *The Wealth of Nations*, Book. 2, Chapter 3 and Book 5, Chapter 1, Part 2, Edwin Cannan (ed.), University of Chicago, Chicago, 1976, Vol. 1, pg. 352, Vol. 2 pgs. 242-43.

36   Maxwell Bloomfield, *American Lawyers in a Changing Society: 1776-1876*, Harvard University Press, Cambridge, 1976, pgs. 39-40.

37 J.B. McMaster, *History of the People of the United States*, Vol. I, quoted in Warren, *A History of the American Bar*, pg. 216.

38 Jefferson, in a letter to Thomas Cooper, 1810, quoted in Mencken, *New Dictionary of Quotations*, pg. 620.

39 Thomas Jefferson, *Writings*, Vol. 1, pg. 86, from Stevenson, *The Home Book of Quotations*, pg. 1093.

40 Herbert V. Prochnow and Herbert V. Prochnow, Jr., *A Treasury of Humorous Quotations*, Harper & Row, New York, 1969, pg. 190.

41 Warren, *A History of the American Bar*, pg. 215.

42 In *The Federalist*, 1788, from Mencken, *New Dictionary of Quotations*, pg. 659.

43 Quoted in Warren, *A History of the American Bar*, pg. 217; and in Friedman, *A History of American Law*, pg. 304.

44 John G. Wells, *Every Man His Own Lawyer*, A.L. Bancroft and Co., New York.

45 Benjamin Austin (Honestus), *Observations on the Pernicious Practice of the Law*, quoted in Roscoe Pound, *The Lawyer from Antiquity to Modern Times*, pgs. 233-34.

46 "What's New," *Americans for Legal Reform*, Vol. 7, No. 3, April/June 87, pg. 28.

47 David P. Szatmary, *Shays' Rebellion: The Making of an Agrarian Insurrection*, University of Massachussets Press, 1980, pgs. 58-59, 99.

CHAPTER FIVE

THE
EARLY
NINETEENTH
CENTURY

HISTORICAL BRIEF

The Age of Brass

The first half or so of the Nineteenth Century has always been considered by legal scholars to be the Formative Era of American law. The names of John Marshall, Daniel Webster, Lemuel Shaw and other "heroes of the law" echo through unctuous legal histories. Lawyers at the time smugly congratulated themselves on the progress of the profession, but the country as a whole remained unimpressed. Joseph Story, one of these erstwhile legal heroes, ponderously asserted that "the discussion of constitutional questions throws a lustre round the bar, and gives a dignity to its functions which can rarely belong to the profession in any other country."[1] But the more popular sentiment was expressed during the same time by one Jesse Higgins: "God never intended his creature man should be under the necessity to carry a written book in his pocket, or a lawyer by his side, to tell him what is just and lawful; he wrote it on his mind."[2]

PLEADING FOR UNDERSTANDING

Christopher Anstey (1724-1805), was an English poet and satirist. Under the pseudonym The Late J.J.S. Esquire, he wrote a work with the imposing title: *The Pleader's Guide, A Didactic Poem, in Two Parts: Containing the Conduct of a Suit of Law, with the Arguments of Counsellor Bother'um and Counsellor Bore'um in an Action betwixt John-a-Gull, and John-a-Gudgeon, for Assault and Battery, at a late Contested Election,* originally published in 1801. The following selection, from the seventh book of this epic endeavor, is subtitled, "An Episode containing authentic Memoirs of Mr. Surrebutler's professional Career:"

> *Whoe'er has drawn a Special Plea*
> *Has heard of old Tom Tewkesbury,*
> *Deaf as a post, and thick as mustard,*
> *He aim'd at Wit, and bawl'd and bluster'd,*
> *And died a* Nisi prius *Leader—*
> *That Genius was my Special Pleader—*
> *That great man's office I attended*
> *By Hawk and Buzzard recommended,*
> *Attorneys both of wondrous skill*
> *To pluck the goose and drive the Quill;*
> *Three years I sat his smokey room in,*
> *Pens, paper, ink and pounce consuming,*
> *The fourth when* Essoign Day *begun,*
> *Joyful I hail'd th' auspicious Sun,*

"I think we may class the lawyer in the natural history of monsters."

John Keats (1795-1821), English poet [3]

Bade Tewkesbury and Clerk adieu,
(Purification, eight-two)
Of both I wash'd my hands; and though
With nothing for my cash to shew,
But Precedents so scrawl'd and blurr'd,
I scarce could read one single word,
Nor in my Books of Common Place
One feature of the Law could trace,
Save Buzzard's nose and visage thin
And Hawk's deficiency of chin,
Which I while lolling at my ease
Was wont to draw instead of Pleas;
My chambers I equipt complete,
Made Friends, hir'd Books, and gave to eat; . . .

But if while capering at my Glass,
Or toying with some fav'rite Lass,
I heard th'aforesaid Hawk a-coming,
Or Buzzard in the staircase humming,
At once the fair angelic maid
Into my coal-hole I convey'd,
At once, with serious look profound
Mine eyes commercing with the ground,
I see'd like one estrang'd to sleep,
"And fix'd in cogitation deep,"
Sat motionless, and in my hand I
Held my Doctrina Placitandi,
And though I never read a page in't,
Thanks to my shrewd, well-judging Agent,
My Sister's husband, Mr. Shark,
Soon got six Pupils and a Clerk,
Five pupils were my stint, the other
I took to compliment his Mother;
All round me came with ready money
Like Hybla bees surcharg'd with honey,
Which, as they press'd it so genteely,
And begg'd me to accept it freely,
Seemed all so fond of Special Pleading,
And all so certain of succeeding,
I who am always all compliance,
As well to Pupils as to Clients,
Took as genteely as they paid it,
And freely to my purse convey'd it;
That I might practically shew,
And they in special manner know
Ere, they began their Pleas to draw
What an Assumpsit meant in Law—
To wit for divers weight sums
Of **lawful cash** at Pleader's Rooms,
By me said Pleader, as was prudent
Hard and received to use of Student;

In short, I acted as became me,
And where's the Pleader that can blame me?. . . [4]

LEGAL LYRICS

James Smith (1775-1849), an English poet, wrote this epigram about the street in London on which he lived:

In Craven street, Strand, the attorneys find place;
And ten dark coal-barges are moor'd at its base.
Fly Honesty, fly! seek some safer retreat,
There's craft in the river and craft in the street.[5]

ENGLAND EXPECTS EVERY LAWYER TO DO HIS DUTY

At the turn of the Nineteenth Century, British militia were organized to repel the invasion of England Napoleon was planning. In London, these military units were often organized by profession, and the lawyers of the Temple raised a regiment. Once, when King George III was reviewing this newly assembled unit, he summoned its commander, Colonel Erskine, and asked him what his regiment was called. Erskine replied that it as yet had no name, to which His Majesty replied: "Call it the 'Devil's Own.'"[7]

THE UTILITARIAN LOGIC OF LAWYER-HATING

Jeremy Bentham (1748-1832), was the son of a lawyer, educated at Oxford, and although he never entered the Inns of Court or practiced law, he devoted much of his life not only to intense study of the law, but also to its reform. Bentham particularly disliked judges. He once wrote: "To elevate a practicing lawyer to the bench, is as expedient as putting a procuress at the head of a girls' school."[8]

Judicial legislation was one of his pet peeves:

It is the judges that make the common law. Do you
know how they do it? Just as a man makes law for his
dog. When your dog does anything you want to break
him of, you wait till he does it, and then beat him for it.
This is the way you make laws for your dog: and this is
the way judges make law for you and me. They won't
tell a man beforehand what it is he should not do—they
won't so much as allow of his being told: they lie by till

*he has done something which they say he should not
have done, and then they hang him for it.*[9]

PRESIDENTIAL WISDOM

From the diary of John Quincy Adams (1767-1848), lawyer
and the sixth President of the United States:

*I told him that I thought it was law logic—an artificial
system of reasoning exclusively used in courts of justice,
but good for nothing anywhere else . . . The source of all
this pettifogging is, that out of judicial courts the end of
human reasoning is truth or justice, but in them it is
law. Ita lex scripta est, [So the law is written] and there
is no reply. Hence it is my firm belief that, if instead of
the long robes of judges and the long speeches of
lawyers, the suitors of every question debated in the
courts between individuals were led blindfolded up to a
lottery wheel and there bidden to draw, each of them
one or two tickets, one marked Right and the other
Wrong, and execution should issue according to the
sentence of the whole, more substantial justice would be
done than is now dispensed by courts of law.*[11]

> **"To seek redress
> of grievances by
> going to law, is
> like sheep running
> for shelter to a
> bramble bush."**
>
> Lewis W. Dilwyn
> (1778-1855)[10]

WHAT MAN OUGHT NOT TO BE

George Watterston was a Maryland attorney who eventually
became the first Librarian of Congress. Disgusted with the bar,
he wrote a novel entitled *The Lawyer, or Man as He Ought Not to
Be*, which contains the following warning of what Watterston
had come to feel were the inevitable effects of the adversarial
system:

> **"Barrister: A
> person you hire
> when you've
> murdered
> somebody and you
> want it explained
> to the jury in the
> best possible
> light."**
>
> Anonymous

*The practice of the law, it is said, tends to brutalize the
feelings, to subvert the judgment, and to annihilate
every virtuous principle of the human heart. I had not
been long at the bar before I discovered the truth of this
declaration; indeed it cannot possibly have any other
tendency. A lawyer, from the first moment he enters into
business, becomes habituated to scenes of injustice and
oppression; from which, if he possess the smallest particle
of sensibility, he turns at first with disgust and abhor-
rence; but custom soon renders them familiar, and in
process of time, he can view them with the utmost
coolness and indifference. This lamentable consequence
is the perpetual fellowship with dishonesty, and a constant intercourse with villainy, will in time destroy every*

tender emotion and sap by degrees the foundation of the most rigid virtue.[12]

Washington Irving (1783-1859), also studied law early in life, but he was bright enough not to make a career of it. He wrote in the literary magazine *Salmagundi* in 1807:

Young lawyers attend the courts, not because they have business there, but because they have no business anywhere else.[13]

An English counterpart to Irving was Douglas William Jerrold (1803-1857), a frequent contributor to *Punch*, the first great satiric magazine. The law was a favorite target:

The Law is a pretty bird, and has charming wings; it would be quite a bird of paradise if it did not carry such a terrible bill.[14]

and

Law is one of the arts—black arts![15]

LEGAL LYRICS

He saw a lawyer killing a viper
On a dunghill hard by his own stable;
And the Devil smiled, for it put him in mind,
Of Cain and his brother Abel.
Samuel Taylor Coleridge (1772-1834), English poet[17]

"The lawyer is a gentleman who rescues your estate from your enemies —and keeps it to himself."

Henry Peter Brougham
(1778-1868)[16]

OLD HICKORY LEADS THE WAY

In the United States of the late 1820s, the populist senti– ments of Jacksonian democracy naturally militated against the snobbery and obscurantism of lawyers, and early Americans demonstrated a healthy distaste for the legal cabal. John Pitts exhibited this attitude in his *Eleven Numbers Against Lawyer Legislation and Fees at the Bar:*

Many a poor vagrant lives on bread and water, and sleeps in the Penitentiary, that never did half the mischief to society that many of these honorable Esquires have done. And if the flood of vile is not stayed, every other class in community will be consumed with utter destruction. A poor tailor saves a few dollars together over the midnight lamp; and the next morning it is demanded of him by a lawyer to defend him in a case that he is a perfect stranger to. The farmer may delve in brier-beds and swamps until the last drop of sweat exudes from his melting frame, in order to support his family, or to provide for himself in his grey hairs; and the whole of it is demanded the next hour by a lawyer to rescue it from a robber who was detected in stealing it the night before. The pathetic cry of the perishing orphan for bread restrains not the avaricious hand of the attorney; but his ears to the mournful tale are deaf as to the zephyr of a distant clime, that passes unheeded and unknown. Known assassins, high-way robbers, and midnight thieves, are all sustained against justice, with all the eloquence and zeal worthy of a better cause; and all right, nothing wrong! when if the same doings and sayings had been done and expressed by a saint, he would be considered accessory! . . .

Laws and politics, when drifting along their natural channel, are as easily understood as the ordinary transactions of neighbor with neighbor; and if on inspection they are found to be otherwise, it is because they have been perverted from their ancient course, and rendered intricate for speculation. In proof of this I refer you to Washington, Franklin, Wm. Henry Harrison, and a host of others, who never saw a law book; yet whose sayings and doings have immortality won, and established them a character for ability in all departments of state, that shall stand plumed in perpetual day, whilst thousands of jurists shall lie "covered in shameful spewing."[18]

LEGAL LYRICS

To fit up a village with tackle for tillage
Jack Carter he took to the saw.
To pluck and to pillage, the same little village
Tim Gordon he took to the law.

Rhyme found in Nineteenth Century
American schoolbooks[19]

In 1829, the English journalist and Member of Parliament William Cobbett (1763-1835), wrote in his *Advice to Young Men:*

"To set an attorney to work to worry and torment another is a very base act; to alarm his family as well as himself, while you are sitting quietly at home."[21]

THE BAR UNBARED

The first bar associations in the new United States arose in the early decades of the Nineteenth Century as the lawyers banded in an attempt to clean up their images and professionalize. To convince a doubting public, the charters of these groups are full of highblown words enumerating the gentlemanly qualities of the brothers of the bar, their professional responsibilities and the requirements for their training. But a not incidental purpose of the bar was setting minimum fees for services. The "Rules of the Bar of Essex County, Massachussets" written in 1831, include a long schedule of fees and the vow: "We bind ourselves not to receive less fees or compensation than are herein expressed, nor any commutation or substitute therefor." Keep in mind that in this period a worker's wages ranged from $1 to $6 a week:

For libels of Divorce, and appearance for the party, exclusive of costs, not less than. . .$12.00

Petition, &c. for Naturalization, exclusive of court and clerk dues, not less than. . .$12.00

Pleas on any issue of fact or law, not less than. . .$10.00

Advice, in any case, not less than; . . .$3.00

Although price-fixing and collusion by businesses has never been tolerated by the courts, lawyers' minimum fee schedules were a fixture of the American legal profession for another 140 years, until finally ruled illegal by the U.S. Supreme Court in 1975.[20]

"A piece of paper, blown by the wind into a law court may in the end only be drawn out again by two oxen."

Chinese Proverb

THE VOICE OF EXPERIENCE

All the attorneys I have ever seen have the same manner: hard, cold, incredulous, distrustful, sarcastic, sneering. They are said to be conversant with the worst part of human nature, and with most discreditable transactions. They have so many falsehoods told them, that they place confidence in no one.

Lord Melbourn (William Lamb) (1779-1848), Prime Minister of England[22]

JUDGING JUDGES

Mr. Serjeant Arabin was a judge at the Old Bailey in the 1830s. The following exchange occurred in one of his trials:

Prisoner: I want to ask whether it is likely—

Arabin: We have nothing to do with what is likely or unlikely: so many unlikely things happen in courts of justice that public time must not be wasted on such enquiries.[23]

THE DELAY OF THE LAW

Half-Centuries of Hubbub

In 1843, the Scottish historian, biographer and social critic Thomas Carlyle (1795-1881), published *Past and Present*, in which he wrote:

The man in horsehair wig advances, promising that he will get me "justice:" he takes me into chancery Law-Courts, into decades, half-centuries of hubbub, of distracted jargon; and does get me—disappointment, almost desperation; and one refuge: that of dismissing him and his "justice" altogether out of my head.[24]

Seward's Folly

William Henry Seward (1801-1872), who became Lincoln's Secretary of State, and is best known for purchasing Alaska from Russia, tried his first civil case in chancery in 1823. This very same case was also the last one Seward ever argued in the Court of Chancery, some twenty-three years later, just before the court was abolished in 1846.[25]

WHAT WILL THEY DO FOR AN ENCORE?

The Spectator, an English newspaper, drew on a recurring theme when it suggested in 1849 that it might be better to transfer the courts to the theatres, "which would be more convenient in more ways than one; the judge, counsel and other performers would welcome the better ventilation; the orchestra would be at hand to accompany Mr. Charles Wilkins and other eloquent gentlemen in the chanting parts of the oratory."[26]

DOING ONE'S BEST

The following anecdote, involving Rufus Choate (1799-1859), a famous American lawyer and senator, describes the ethics of legal greed:

> *A lawyer, on being called to account by Rufus Choate for having acted unprofessionally in taking less than the usual fee from his client, pleaded that he had taken all the man had.*
>
> *"Very well," said Mr. Choate, "We will have to excuse you, then."*[27]

ON THE LACK OF DEMOCRACY IN THE LAWYERS' AMERICA

Alexis de Tocqueville (1805-1859), the French politician and writer, wrote his *On Democracy in America* from observations made while on a government mission to study the American penal system. He had much to report about lawyers, laws and judges:

"There are three sorts of lawyers— able, unable and lamentable."

Robert Smith Surtees, English humorist (1803-1864)[28]

> *The courts of justice are the visible organs by which the legal profession is enabled to control democracy. The judge is a lawyer who works with lawyers to maintain the* status quo *—and aggressively denounces and works against legal reform that would strengthen the constitutional rights of the American people. Lawyers are united in their common interests and intent to maintain the* status quo *at all times. Lawyers prize and value legality more than they value freedom.*[29]

MORE THAN JUST A NAME, IT'S A WAY OF LIFE

The word "shyster" appears to have originated in New York around 1840. It derives from the name of a lawyer Scheuster, pronounced "Shoister," whose behavior in court so angered Justice Osborne of the Essex Market Police Court that he took to rebuking other lawyers for "Scheuster practices."[30]

SELF-RELIANCE

In the early years of the Republic, most people lived in rural areas remote from cities and lawyers. As a result, many laypeople practiced law. And the country prospered notwithstanding. The following is from Thomas Wooler's *Every Man His*

Own Attorney, published in 1845, one of many self-help manuals:

> *When attorneys are employed, they must be paid; and their charges are not always regulated whether by their abilities or their services to a client, but by their own desire to make as much as they can. This evil can only be remedied by making their clients well informed on common subjects, and able to see what course they are taking in matters of more intricacy.*[31]

THE PURPLED MOUNTAINS UNLAWYERED MAJESTY

> *The trappers say there is more real pleasure in one year in the mountains than a whole lifetime in a dense, settled country. There are no political pursuits to tire and weary, and last but not least, no law or lawyers to pettifog among them or mar their peace and sew discord among them.*

Richard May, in 1848 [32]

HOW TO COOK A GOOSE, LEGALLY

Throughout the history of the United States, and well before, the experience that black Americans have had with the legal system has hardly served to impress them with its justice or impartiality. This attitude is reflected in the following African-American folktale:

> *One day Brother Fox caught Brother Goose and tied him to a tree.*
>
> *"I'm going to eat you, Br'er Goose," he said, "You've been stealing my meat."*
>
> *"But I don't even eat meat." Br'er Goose protested.*
>
> *"Tell that to the judge and jury," said Br'er Fox.*
>
> *"Who's gonna be the judge?" asked Br'er Goose.*
>
> *"A fox," answered Br'er Fox.*
>
> *"And who's gonna be the jury?" Br'er Goose inquired.*

"They all gonna be foxes," said Br'er Fox, grinning so all his teeth showed.

"Guess my goose is cooked," sighed Br'er Goose.[33]

"When the lawyer acts according to his conscience the blind man will believe what his eyes see."

German Proverb[36]

PRESIDENTIAL WISDOM

Abraham Lincoln (1808-1865), was a lawyer, but he was known to turn his incorrigible wit in the direction of his brethren-in-law. Speaking of another lawyer, he once said:

He can compress the most words into the smallest idea of any man I ever met.[34]

On another occasion, he advised:

Discourage litigation. Persuade your neighbors to compromise whenever you can. Point out to them how the nominal winner is often a real loser in fees, expenses and waste of time.[35]

NOT SUCH BON MOTS

Charles Caleb Colton (1782-1836) wrote:

Lawyers are the only civil delinquents whose judges must of necessity be chosen from themselves.[37]

and

Pettifoggers in law and empirics in medicine, whether their patients lose or save their property or their lives, take care to be, in either case, equally remunerated; they profit by both horns of the dilemma, and press defeat no less than success into their service.[38]

and

In civil jurisprudence it too often happens that there is so much law, that there is no room for justice, and that the claimant expires of wrong in the midst of right, as mariners die of thirst in the midst of water.[39]

SIMILES OF THE LAW

Law is like a country dance; people are led up and down in it till they are fairly tired out; it is like a book of surgery, there are a great many terrible cases in it; it is like a physic too, they that take the least of it are best off; it is like a homely gentleman, very well to follow, and like a scolding wife, very bad when it follows us; it is like a new fashion, people are bewitched to get into it, and like bad weather, most people are glad to get out of it.

John Sterling (1806-1844), Scotch-Irish writer[40]

"The animals are not so dumb as is thought: they have no lawyers."

Anonymous

ROGUES GALLERY

Edwin James (1812-1882)

In the Victorian period, many English barristers gained fame not through their legal knowledge, but rather through their courtroom performance. Actors and barristers often went to the same training schools. Many well-known lawyers of this era had actually worked as actors in their youth, and the most infamous of these was Edwin James. If James had stayed on the stage, he may not have climbed so high, but he certainly would not have fallen so low.

In 1847, James became involved in his first, though by no means his last, political scandal. The Attorney-General Sir John Jervis wanted his twenty-one year-old son to take up a career, so he decided to buy him a seat in Parliament. He picked Horsham as his son's seat, and retained James as his agent in the borough. The job of such agents was, primarily, to bribe the voters. This bribery usually took the form of providing free food and drink for the few weeks preceding the campaign to hungry and thirsty locals—although cash payments were certainly not unknown. As J.R. Lewis observed in *The Victorian Bar.*

The unscrupulous lawyer-agent would certainly not lose money during the campaign and could well obtain for himself an entry into the more fashionable homes in London thereafter. And some, like Edwin James, used the favour they obtained to batten on the family later— obtaining huge loans of money that were never repaid.[41]

James was a good agent, at least in the sense that young Jervis won his seat. But the Horsham contest was challenged. While this was standard procedure, the fact that the Attorney-General was involved raised some eyebrows. A deal was struck:

The election would be declared void; in return, bribery charges would not be brought. As part of the deal, James offered to pay the challengers 1,500 pounds "towards costs"—in other words, a bribe. But after the charges were dropped, Jervis and James refused to pay. The abused party, a man named Newmarch, was furious and pressed thirty-two bribery charges against the Attorney-General and James.

Brethren of the bench and bar, of course, rallied for James and Jervis. Behind-the-scenes machinations ensured that *Newmarch vs. James* was tried before the *Jervis* case—in which there was more incriminating evidence. Fitzroy Kelly, who represented James, called the action a "cruel nefarious attempt to destroy the reputation of a respectable and honest man" and the judge agreed, finding for defendant James.

James became a Queen's Counsel in 1850 after fifteen years as a junior barrister. There was a great deal of prestige in "taking the silk" and an added advantage was that a QC could charge higher fees. James enthusiastically pursued his opportunities.

One of the most lucrative areas of Victorian practice was representing petitions to the Election Committees of the House of Commons. The fact that he had shamelessly engaged in bribery did not stop James from becoming a member of the group of lawyers who specialized in preparing and presenting these petitions, and he made a great deal of money. In 1856, he handled nineteen petitions at the same time—and his income in that year went up from 6,000 to 12,000 pounds at a time when a judge earned 5,000 pounds a year.

In 1859, James ran for election to the House of Commons from Marylebone. It cost him 6,000 pounds in legitimate expenses and almost 20,000 pounds in bribes. Costs were high because the election was successfully challenged. James had to run again, and his voters insisted on being bought anew.

Although a wealthy man, James consistently lived beyond his means, financing his imbroglios by borrowing from moneylenders and wealthy acquaintances. His increasing indebtedness made him even less scrupulous than usual about the source of his income. In a trial in 1860, it was rumored that he took 1,500 pounds from the opposing side to compromise his client's case. When he abruptly changed sides in another case, it led to an investigation by the Benchers of the Inner Temple, senior members of the Inns of Court. It was revealed that James had defrauded friends, lawyers and lovers to the tune of 100,000 pounds.

When talk of disbarment began, James married a rich widow and hightailed it to America. He was disbarred and stripped of his QC *in absentia*. But he had found the land of endless opportunity. In New York, he resumed not only his legal career, but his acting as well, playing to both courtrooms and the prestigious Winter Garden. He returned to England in 1872, lecturing, writing and hiring himself out as a consultant. He died in London on March 4, 1882.

"It is the business of the lawyer to find a hole to creep out of any law which is in his way; and if there is no hole, to make one."

Sir William Ouseley
(1771-1842)[42]

SELECTIONS FROM A MASTER

Charles Dickens (1812-1870)

Dickens was born at Portsmouth, the son of a naval clerk. In many of his novels, he wrote knowingly of the law; he worked as a court reporter at the age of seventeen. Much of the most famous and beloved anti-lawyeriana flowed from his pen:

Oliver Twist, Chapter 51

The following exchange between Mr. Bumble and the lawyer Brownlow provides a well-known, if often misspelled, quotation:

"It was all Mrs. Bumble. She would do it," urged Mr. Bumble; first looking round to ascertain that his partner had left the room.

"That is no excuse," replied Mr. Brownlow. "You were present on the occasion of the destruction of these trinkets, and indeed the more guilty of the two, in the eye of the law; for the law supposes that your wife acts under your direction."

"If the law suppose that," said Mr. Bumble, squeezing his hat emphatically in both hands, "the law is a ass—a idiot."[43]

Pickwick Papers, Chapter 20

Mr. Pickwick, on a visit to the office of some particularly sleazy lawyers, is prevented from striking one of them by his friend Mr. Weller, who urges discretion as the better part of valor:

"You just come avay," said Mr. Weller. "Battledore and shuttlecock's a wery good game, vhen you a'n't the shuttlecock and two lawyers the battledore, in wich case it gets too excitin' to be pleasant."[44]

Battledore and shuttlecock is now known as badminton.

Bleak House, Chapter 1

Fog everywhere. Fog up the river, where it flows among green aits and meadows; fog down the river, where it rolls defiled among the tiers of shipping and the waterside pollutions of a great (and dirty) city. Fog on the Essex marshes, fog on the Kentish heights. Fog creeping into the cabooses of collier-brigs, fog lying out on the yards, and hovering in the rigging of great ships; fog drooping on the gunwales of barges and small boats...

The raw afternoon is rawest, and the dense fog is densest, and the muddy streets are muddiest, near that leaden-headed old obstruction, appropriate ornament for the threshold of a leaden-headed old corporation: Temple Bar. And hard by Temple Bar, in Lincoln's Inn Hall, at the very heart of the fog, sits the Lord High Chancellor in his High Court of Chancery.

Never can there come fog too thick, never can there come mud and mire too deep, to assort with the groping and floundering condition which this High Court of Chancery, most pestilent of hoary sinners, holds, this day, in the sight of heaven and earth.

On such an afternoon, if ever, the Lord High Chancellor ought to be sitting here—as here he is—with a foggy glory round his head, softly fenced in with crimson cloth and curtains, addressed by a large advocate with great whiskers, a little voice, and an interminable brief, and outwardly directing his contemplation to the lantern in the roof, where he can see nothing but fog. On such an afternoon, some score of members of the High Court of Chancery bar ought to be—as here they are—mistily engaged in one of the ten thousand stages of an endless cause, tripping one another up on slippery precedents, groping knee-deep in technicalities, running their goat-hair and horse-hair warded heads against walls of words, and making a pretence of equity with serious faces, as players might. On such an afternoon, the various solicitors in the cause, some two or three of whom have inherited it from their fathers, who made a fortune by it, ought to be—as are they not?—ranged in a line, in a long matted well (but you might look in vain for Truth at the bottom of it), between the registrar's red table and the silk gowns, with bills, cross-bills, answers, rejoinders, injunctions, affidavits, issues, references to masters, masters' reports, mountains of costly nonsense, piled before them . . . . This is the Court of Chancery . . . which so exhausts finances, patience, courage, hope; so overthrows the brain and breaks the heart; that there is not an honourable man among its practitioners who would not give— who does not often give—the warning, "Suffer any wrong that can be done you rather than come here!"[45]

THE DELAY OF THE LAW

In 1852, the case of *Beckford vs. Jasper*, begun 104 years earlier, was finally settled. The seeds of this case were sown in 1748 when Beckford's executor filed a 10,000 pound estate. The actual proceeding began in 1753 before Lord Chancellor Hardwicke, and when it was settled nearly a century later, the estate had grown to 70,000 pounds. No one has ever calculated the amount taken by generations of lawyers from this estate. The interminable case immortalized by Charles Dickens as *Jarndyce and Jarndyce* in *Bleak House* seems to have been the William Jennings case, which though unsettled when Dickens started writing in 1852, had been going on for a mere fifty-four years.[46]

"He fareth best who loveth best All fees both great and small. For the Bench declare that etiquette Of the Bar is 'Pocket All.' "

Punch, 1847[47]

RUNNING FROM OFFICE

After the Parliamentary Reform Act of 1832, the first of a number of reforms that democratized English elections, many lawyers rushed to get themselves voted into the House of Commons. There were seventy-five lawyers in the House by 1852. Disraeli referred to the "importunate barristers" as part of the "vagabond population" of Parliament. These barristerial politicians did not meet with overwhelming approval from the electorate, either. When Charles Wilkins appeared at the hustings in Southhampton in 1856, he was met with the heckling cries: "No lawyers, no lawyers!"

The crowd stormed the podium, and the candidate had to flee.[48]

NOTES

1 Charles M. Haar (ed.), *The Golden Age of American Law*, George Braziller, NewYork, 1965, pg. 4.

2 Quoted in Maxwell Bloomfield, *American Lawyers in a Changing Society: 1776-1876*, Harvard University Press, Cambridge, 1976, pg. 48.

3 John Keats, in a letter to George and Georgiana Keats written in 1819, from H.L. Mencken, *A New Dictionary of Quotations on Historical Principles*, Alfred E. Knopf, New York, 1942, pg. 667.

4 Christopher Anstey, *The Pleader's Guide, A Didactic Poem, in Two Parts: Containing the Conduct of a Suit of Law, with the Arguments of Counsellor Bother'um and Counsellor Bore'um in an Action betwixt John-a-Gull, and John-a-Gudgeon, for Assault and Battery, at a late Contested Election*, 4th Edition, London, 1804, pgs. 77-83.

5 Irving Browne, *Law and Lawyers in Literature*, Soule and Bugbee, Boston, 1883, (reprinted by Wm. W. Gaunt and Sons, Inc., Holmes Beach, Florida, 1982), pgs. 299-300.

6 W.H. Auden and Louis Kronenberger, *The Viking Book of Aphorisms*, Viking, New York, 1966, pg. 207.

7 James M. Beck, *May It Please the Court*, Books for Libraries Press, Freeport, New York, 1st publication, 1930, reprinted in 1970, pg. 91.

8 William Seagle, *Men of the Law: From Hammurabi to Holmes*, Macmillan, New York, 1947, pg. 255.

9 Seagle, *Men of the Law*, pg. 256.

10 Tryon Edwards, *Useful Quotations*, Grosset & Dunlap, New York, 1936, pg. 325.

11 Diary of John Quincy Adams, Vol. IV, quoted in Charles Warren, *A History of the American Bar*, Little, Brown, Boston, 1911 (reprinted by William S. Hein, Buffalo, NY, 1980), pg. 382.

12 *The Lawyer or Man as he ought not to be*, pg. 55, from Bloomfield, *American Lawyers in a Changing Society: 1776-1876*, pg. 170.

13 Washington Irving, *Salmagundi* June 27, 1807, pg. 667.

14 Day, *Day's Collacon*, pg. 494.

15 Day, *Day's Collacon*, pg. 493.

16 (attributed) W. Gurney Benham, *Benham's Book of Quotations*, Cassell & Co., New York, 1907, pg. 29a.

17   Samuel Coleridge, "The Devil's Thoughts" quoted in Browne, *Law and Lawyers in Literature*, pg. 256.

18   John W. Pitts, *Eleven Numbers against Lawyer Legislation and Fees at the Bar*, 1843, quoted in Haar (ed.), *The Golden Age of American Law*, pgs. 46-7.

19   Quoted in Ruth Miller Elson, *Guardians of Tradition:: American Schoolbooks of the Nineteenth Century*, University of Nebraska Press, Lincoln, 1964, pg. 26.

20   "Rules of the Bar of the County of Essex, Massachusetss" (1831) quoted in Haar (ed.), *The Golden Age of American Law*, pg. 87.

21   Mencken, *New Dictionary of Quotations*, pg. 665.

22   From Martin Mayer, *The Lawyers*, Harper & Row, New York, 1967, pg. 3.

23   Stephen Tumim, *Great Legal Fiascos*, Arthur Barker, London, 1985, pgs. 115-16.

24   Thomas Carlyle, *Past and Present: Chartism and Sartor Resartus*, Harper & Brothers, New York, pg. 261.

25   *Seward's Life*, D. Appleton & Co., New York, 1877, Vol. 1, pgs. 97-9; quoted in George Martin, *Causes and Conflicts: The Centennial History of the Association of the Bar of the City of New York 1870-1970*, Houghton Mifflin Co., Boston, 1970, pg. 300.

26   J.R. Lewis, *The Victorian Bar*, Robert Hale, London, 1982, pg 14.

27   Eli Perkins (ed.), *Wit and Humor of the Age*, Ross Publishing House, Albany (NY), 1889, pg. 395.

28   Robert Surtees, *Plain or Ringlets*, Chapter 25, Quoted in Benham's *Book of Quotations*, pg. 373b.

29   Alexis de Tocqueville, *Democracy in America* (1851); quoted by V. Corsetti, *Nolo News*, Spring, 1987, pg. 10

30   Richard H. Rovere, *Howe and Hummel*, Farrar Straus & Giroux, New York, 1947, 1974, pg. 10.

31   John G. Wells, *Every Man His Own Lawyer*, A.L. Bancroft and Co., New York.

32   "Short Takes," *Nolo News*, Spring, 1986, pg. 6, from J.S. Holliday, *The World Rushed In*, Simon & Schuster, New York, 1981.

33   "His Goose Is Cooked," *Nolo News*, Summer, 1985, pg. 3.

34   Benham, *Benham's Quotations*, pg. 125a.

35   In *Notes for a Law Lecture*, July 1, 1850 from Bruce Bohle, *The Home Book of American Quotations*, Dodd, Mead and Co., New York, 1967, pg. 226.

36   Robert Christy, *Proverbs, Maxims and Phrases*, G.P. Putnam's Sons, New York, 1907, pg. 612.

37   In *Lacon*, 1820, from Mencken, *New Dictionary of Quotations*, pg. 667.

38   Edwards, *Useful Quotations*, pg. 329.

39   Edwards, *Useful Quotations*, pg. 328.

40   Day, *Day's Collacon*, pg. 494.

41   Lewis, *The Victorian Bar*, pg. 56.

42   Day, *Day's Collacon*, pg. 496.

43   Charles Dickens, *Oliver Twist*, Chapter 51, Dodd, Mead & Co., New York, 1984, pgs. 519-20.

44   Dickens, *Pickwick Papers*, Chapter 20, Oxford University Press, London, 1967, pg. 269.

45   Dickens, *Bleak House*, (1853) Chapter 1 "In Chancery" Norton Edition (George Ford, Sylvere Mondon, eds.), pgs. 5-6.

46   Dickens, *Bleak House*, Norton Edition, pgs. xviii and 888.

47   Lewis, *The Victorian Bar*, pg. 43.

48   Lewis, *The Victorian Bar,* pgs. 54-7.

CHAPTER SIX

THE
LATE
NINETEENTH
CENTURY

HISTORICAL BRIEF

Lawyers Manifest Their Destiny

The appearance of the great railroad ventures provided American lawyers with the first taste of the gravy train called corporate law. Most, of course, still delight in riding it. Before the Civil War, a law firm of more than two or three was practically unheard of, and a lawyer on salary with a corporation unknown. But by the closing quarter of the century, the railroads, insurance companies and Wall Street offered a comfortable living for many lawyers.

Whereas lawyers and firms once lived off making wills, collecting debts and transferring real estate, the new legal breed worked on corporate organization and reorganization, corporate securities, floating bonds and deal-making. These changes brought about a new fee system. Previously, lawyers charged for services rendered. But the new corporate lawyer was on a long-term retainer, and got paid whether working or not. Free at last. No more scratching about for business or enduring lean times. No more time and energy devoted to the courtroom. The new lawyer became less a hired gun and more a hired hand—someone who scoured the dusty tomes of the law to find the exceptions, qualifications, refutations and misprints that would allow a corporate sponsor to exploit and monopolize. Lawyers could thus easily avoid the risks of the courtroom altogether.

More and more lawyers took the path enjoyed by the unnamed Wall Street attorney of Melville's "Bartleby the Scrivener"—"one of those unambitious lawyers who never address a jury, or in any way draw down public applause; but, in the cool tranquillity of a snug retreat, do a snug business....Or, as the more brash creation of Finley Peter Dunne, Mr. Dooley, put it:

> What wud I be doin' in a smelly coort room talkin' up to a man that was me chief clerk last year?' says he. "No, sir, th' law is a diff'rent profissyon fr'm what it was whin Dan'l Webster an' Rufus Choate an' thim gas bags used to make a mighty poor livin' be shoutin' at judges that made less. Th' law today is not only a profissyon. It's a business. I made a bigger honoraryum last year consolodatin' th' glue interests that afterwards wint into th' hands iv a receiver, which is me, t'hin Dan'l Webster iver thought was in th' goold mines iv th' wurruld. I can't promise to take a case fr y an' hoot me reasons fr thinkin' ye're right into th' ears iv a larned judge. I'm a poor speaker. But if iver ye want to do something ye think ye oughtn't to do, come around to me an' I'll show ye how to do it," says he.[1]

JUDGING JUDGES

James T. Brady (1815-1869), was one of the best lawyers of his day. He tried fifty-two murder cases and lost only one. He was under no illusions about the legal ability of many of the judges he faced. Once, when he pleaded a client's ignorance of the law in extenuation of an offense he had committed, the following exchange occurred:

> *Judge*: *Every man is presumed to know the law, Mr. Brady.*

> *Brady*: *I am aware of that, your honor. Every shoemaker, tailor, mechanic and illiterate laborer is presumed to know the law; every man is presumed to know it except the judges . . . and we have a court of appeals to correct their mistakes.*[2]

"Possession is nine points of the law and lawyers' fees are the other ninety-one points."

Anonymous

WHEN RAKISHNESS PAYS OFF

One of the leading lights of the Victorian bench and bar was Sir Alexander Cockburn (1802-1880), a man with a well-deserved reputation for high living and recklessness. As a youth he was a gambler and philanderer, and almost always in debt. He did not change his habits as he matured. When he was initially put forward for a peerage, Queen Victoria rejected him after discovering he had been carrying on with the wife of a Cambridge greengrocer, with whom he had three children.

It was said that as Attorney-General he still went on circuit with Lady Cockburn, but a different one each time. Perhaps despite this lack of scruples, but more probably because of it, he achieved great success in his chosen profession—eventually rising to Lord Chief Justice of England. In his early years, he was particularly adept in the lawyerly art of courtroom acting.

Sir Alexander Cockburn was once spoken of by an enthusiastic juror in these terms:

> *In my time I have heard Sir Alexander in pretty nearly every part. I have heard him as an old man and a young woman; I have heard him when he has been a ship run down at sea, and when he had been an oil-factory in a state of conflagration. Once, when I was foreman of a jury, I saw him poison his most intimate friend, and another time he did the part of a pious bank director in a fashion that would have skinned the eyelids of Exeter Hall. He ain't bad as a desolate widow with nine children, of which the eldest is under eight years of age; but, if ever I have to listen to him again, I should like to see him as a young lady of good*

connections who has been seduced by an officer in the Guards.[3]

Keeping the Lamp Lit

Like the English Puritans and the early American Colonists, the brave pioneers who settled the Western wilderness hoped to establish a new society without the civilizin' influence of lawyers. During the early settlement of Colorado, the territory was divided into mining districts—each of which promulgated its own laws. The sentiments of the settlers are obvious in the following edicts:

> ***Trail Creek District, Aug. 20, 1860****: No lawyer, attorney, counselor, or pettifogger shall be allowed to plead in any case or before any judge or jury in this district.*

> ***Banner District, March 8, 1861****: No lawyer or pettifogger shall be allowed to plead in any court in this district.*

> ***Lower Union District, Revision of March, 1861, Sec. 9****: Resolved, That no lawyer shall be permitted to practice law in any court in this district, under penalty of not more than fifty, nor less than twenty lashes, and be banished from the district.*[5]

No Bacon

One reason that lawyers were so unpopular in the American West is indicated in this item which appeared in the *Cheyenne Leader,* a paper in frontier Wyoming:

> *Four sheep, a hog and ten bushels of wheat settled an Iowa breach of promise suit where $25,000 damages were demanded. The lawyers got all but the hog, which died before they could drive it away.*[6]

The One Great Principle of Law

James Hurnard (1800-1881), an Englishman once described in a biography as a "Victorian character," wrote this about lawyers in his poem "The Setting Sun," published in 1871:

> *If you simply buy a house,*
> *He will take note of every interview,*
> *And charge you for receiving your instructions,*

Charge you likewise for drawing up the same—
Eight folio pages with a world of margin;
Charge you likewise for copying the same,
Charge you likewise for reading you the same,
And reading of it to the other party;
Charge you likewise for reading long reply
From Finden, the lawyer, with a draft agreement;
Charge you likewise perusing said draft;
Charge you likewise transmitting draft agreement.[7]

THE EVER-WAXING BAR

In 1870, there were 40,000 lawyers in the United States—1.06 per 1,000 people; in 1900, there were 114,460—1.51 per 1,000. California was cursed with nearly twice as many as the country as a whole. Between 1870 and 1900, California's legal population grew by 165 percent; but the legal profession nearly tripled. There were 1,115 lawyers in the state in 1870, or 1.99 per 1,000; there were 4,278 in 1900, or 2.88 per 1,000.[9]

> *"First I charge a retainer; then I charge a reminder; next I charge a refresher; and then I charge a finisher."*
>
> Judah P. Benjamin (1811-1884), lawyer and Confederate statesman[8]

LEGAL LYRICS

Out of the Mouths of Babes

The children's song "Pop Goes The Weasel" is famous, but lawyers figure in one of its lesser-known verses:

I went to a lawyer today,
For something very legal,
He asked me how much I'm willing to pay—
Pop goes the weasel!
I will bargain all my days,
But never again so feeble,
I paid for ev'ry legal phrase,
Pop goes the weasel![10]

ROGUES GALLERY

William Howe (1828-1902) and Abraham Hummel (1849-1926)

In the last quarter or so of the Nineteenth Century, William "The Weeper" Howe and Abraham "Little Abie," or more poetically, "The Light of the Tenderloin" Hummel were the most notorious, scurrilous, audacious—and popular—lawyers of their

day. Even in the debased coinage of the time, Howe and Hummel had national reputations as shameless but brilliant scoundrels. Between their organization as a law firm in 1869 and their ignominious demise in 1907, their skill in satisfying clients—whether by embracing justice or banishing it at the threshold of the courtroom with technicalities, half-truths, perjury, or bribes—was a source of incredulity and admiration.

They were hardly content to make due with mere rhetoric or law. They had on call a cast of professional witnesses, and could produce a weepy young mother or orphaned child in no time. Stronger medicine was used as needed. When Judge Albert Cordozo, one of Tweed's corrupt magistrates, went on trial, it was discovered that he had accepted bribes on behalf of over two hundred Howe and Hummel clients. In one civil suit, they represented both plaintiff and defendant.

Howe was the elder of the two, a robust and flamboyant man given to a highly personal wardrobe of dark purple or green waistcoats, checkered pants and unsubtle jewelry. "When engaged in the trial of a celebrated case," related his obituary, "he would often change his clothing for every session of the court . . . . Diamonds in clusters, horseshoes, sunbursts and other forms adhered to the person of Mr. Howe wherever it was possible to place them."[11]

Howe's success did not lie in book-learning, but in his bombastic, high-Victorian courtroom delivery. "He was the most accomplished weeper of his day," said contemporary Samuel Hopkins Adams. "He could and would cry over any case, no matter how commonplace. His voice would quaver, his jowls would quiver, his great shoulders would shake, and presently authentic tears would well up in his bulbous eyes and dribble over. It was a sickening spectacle, but it often carried a jury to extraordinary conclusions."[12] Howe would strut, kneel, grimace, or beg, as the occasion demanded. He once delivered a three-hour-long summation entirely on his knees.

And he found the perfect partner in Abe Hummel, his opposite in every way—except greed. "Little Abie" was short and slouched, with birdlike limbs and a huge head. In contrast to the motley Howe, Hummel dressed almost always in black. "He looks like an abortion," said client Stanford White.

His contribution to the firm was a steeltrap legal mind that could always find just the right technical flaw or legal cranny to set one or another of the firm's disreputable clients free. When those didn't do the trick, Hummel would just go around the law. He did a great deal of divorce work, regularly and without remorse using perjured testimony and professional co-respondents. To his profitable law practice, Hummel added a thriving sideline—blackmail, a racket he ran practically like an assembly line. He would find a seduced and abandoned young woman, make out an affidavit of breach of promise, and then offer to "sell" the document to the gentleman in question for a fee ranging from $5 to $10,000. He pulled off this trick upwards of 500 times, and it was an open secret in New York, particularly among the theatrical crowd, where many chorus girls favored its use.

Howe and Hummel served as the unofficial bar of the New York underworld. The most notorious of New York's criminal element were satisfied clients of the firm: the infamous fence Mother Mandelbaum, the superlative counterfeiter Charles O. Brockway, bank robber George Leonidas Leslie, the Sheeny Mob, the Whyos Gang, all the major policy-shop owners and bookmakers and a large number of the city's amateur and professional desperadoes. When seventy-four brothel owners were rounded up during a reform drive in 1884, every one turned out to be a Howe and Hummel client. And in January of 1873, of the twenty-five prisoners awaiting trial in the Tombs for murder or manslaughter, all but two were their clients.

Many of the nation's most well-known individuals rubbed shoulders with the riff-raff in the Howe and Hummel waiting room. The firm represented the boxer John L. Sullivan, actors John Barrymore and Edwin Booth (the brother of Lincoln's assassin), actresses Lillian Russell and Lillian Langtry, P.T. Barnum, Stanford White and other folks—some of whom were quite respectable.

The firm reached its peak at the end of the Nineteenth Century, but barely survived into the Twentieth. Howe died in 1902. Hummel was only fifty-three at the time of his partner's death, but his lawyerly days were numbered. In 1907, after a four-year struggle with the reform-minded District Attorney William Travers Jerome, Hummel was convicted of suborning perjury and sentenced to a year in prison—there, no doubt, to rub elbows with many former clients. Immediately after his release, Hummel retired to Europe, and died, forgotten, in London in 1926.[13]

A POX ON YOUR HOUSE

Henry Wheeler Shaw (1818-1885), who wrote under the name of Josh Billings, didn't think much of the law or lawyers. Before he started his writing career he had been a real estate broker, and it was as true then as now that brokers think of lawyers as, at best, a necessary evil and at worst, not necessary at all.

Wrote Shaw:

*Every man should know something of the law. If he
knows enough to keep out of it, he's a pretty good
lawyer.*[14]

HIGHFLOWN JUSTICE

The following epigram is said to have been written on a
wall of the New York City Hall, the dome of which is topped by
a figure of Justice:

*The lawyers all, both great and small,
Come here to cheat the people;
For be it known that justice's flown,
And perches on the steeple.*[15]

CLEMENS-Y FOR THE LAWYER

Mark Twain (1835-1910), one of the greatest American hu-
morists, could hardly have been expected to spare such inviting
targets as lawyers and the law. A couple of his choicest remarks
include:

*To succeed in the other trades, capacity must be shown;
in the law, concealment of it will do.*[16]

And then there is this choice remark from his essay "On the
Decay of the Art of Lying" published in 1882, in which he
observed:

*What chance has the ignorant, uncultivated liar
against the educated expert? What chance have I . . .
against a lawyer?*[17]

And Twain could strike other well-placed blows for the
layperson. At a New England society dinner, he had just finished
a speech when the renowned lawyer William M. Evarts (1818-
1901), arose, shoved both of his hands down into his trouser
pockets, as was his habit, and said: "Doesn't it strike this company as a little unusual that a professional humorist should be
funny?" Twain waited until the laughter excited by this sally had
subsided, and then drawled: "Doesn't it strike this company as a
little unusual that a lawyer should have his hands in his own
pockets?"[18]

LEGAL LYRICS

Lowly Tactics in the Court on High

Fictional lawyers, upon death, generally end up sweating with the devil down below. Here's the versified story, from an anonymous poetaster, of one lawyer who used his legal wiles to gain entry into a more comfortable eternity:

Professions will abuse each other;
The Priest won't call the lawyer brother;
Yet will I readily suppose
They are not truly bitter foes,
But only have their pleasant jokes,
And banter, just like other folks;
As thus—for so they quiz the law—
Once on a time th' Attorney Flaw,
A man, to tell you as the fact is,
Of vast chicane, of course of practice
(But what profession can we trace
Where some will not the corps disgrace?
Seduced, perhaps, by roguish client,
Who tempts him to become more pliant),
A notice had to quit the world,
And from his desk at length was hurled.
Observe, I pray, the plain narration;
'Twas in a hot and long vacation,
When time he had, but no assistance,
Though great from courts of law the distance,
To reach the court of truth and justice
(Where, I confess, my only trust is);
Though here below the learned pleader
Shows talents worthy of a leader,
Yet his own fame he must support,
Be sometimes witty with the court,
Or work the passions of a jury,
By tender strains, or, full of fury,
Misleads them all, though twelve apostles,
While with new law the judge he jostles,
And makes them all give up their powers
To speeches of at least three hours.
But we have left our little man,
And wandered from our purposed plan:
'Tis said (without ill-natured leaven),
"If ever lawyers go to heaven,
It surely is by slow degrees."
(Perhaps 'tis slow they take their fees.)
The case, then, now I'll fairly state:
Flaw reached at last to heaven's high gate:
Quite spent, he rapped; none did it neater;
The gate was opened by St. Peter,

Who looked astonished when he saw,
All black, the little man of law;
But charity was Peter's guide,
For, having once himself denied
His Master, he would not o'erpass
The penitent of any class;
Yet, never having heard there entered
A lawyer, nay, nor one that ventured
Within the realms of peace and love,
He told him, mildly, to remove,
And would have closed the gate of day
Had not old Flaw, in suppliant way,
Demurring to so hard a fate,
Begged but a look, though through the gate.
St. Peter, rather off his guard,
Unwilling to be thought too hard,
Opens the gate to let him peep in.
What did the lawyer? Did he creep in,
Or dash at once to take possession?
Oh no! he knew his own profession;
He took his hat off with respect,
And would no gentle means neglect;
But, finding it was all in vain
For him admittance to obtain,
Thought it were best, let come what will,
To gain an entry by his skill.
So, while St. Peter stood aside
To let the gate be opened wide,
He skimmed his hat with all his strength
Within the gates to no small length.
St. Peter stared; the lawyer asked him
"Only to fetch his hat," and passed him;
But when he reached the jack he'd thrown,
Oh, then was all the lawyer shown;
He clapped it on, and, arms akimbo
(As if he'd been the gallant Bembo),
Cried out, "What think you of my plan?
EJECT ME, PETER, IF YOU CAN.'[20]

ESQ., R.I.P.

An epitaph from a gravestone in St. Pancras churchyard, England:

Here lieth one, deny it if you can,
Who, though a lawyer, was an honest man:
The gates of heav'n to him are opened wide,
But shut, alas! to all the tribe beside.[21]

TWO MANY LAWYERS

In the Nineteenth Century, as today, the courts assigned young lawyers to defend poor defendants. The accused are not always suitably impressed. The American humorist Melville DeLancy Landon (1839-1910), who wrote under a pseudonym, Eli Perkins, related the following story:

> *A judge had appointed two young lawyers to defend an old experienced horse-thief. After inspecting his counsel some time in silence, the prisoner rose in his place and addressed the bench.*
> *"Air them to defend me?"*
> *"Yes, sir," said the judge.*
> *"Both of them?" asked the prisoner.*
> *"Both of them," responded the judge.*
> *"Then I plead guilty," and the poor fellow took his seat and sighed heavily.*[22]

"May your life be filled with lawyers."

Mexican Curse

LEGAL LYRICS

As previously mentioned, Hell is generally held to be chock- full of lawyers, but the anonymous author of "The Devil and The Lawyers" disagreed:

> *The devil came up to the earth one day,*
> *And into the court he wended his way,*
> *Just as the attorney, with a very grave face,*
> *Was proceeding to argue the point in the case.*
>
> *Now, a lawyer his majesty never had seen,*
> *For to his dominions none ever had been,*
> *And he felt very anxious the reason to know,*
> *Why none had been sent to the regions below.*
>
> *'Twas the fault of his agents, his majesty thought*
> *That none of the lawyers had ever been caught,*
> *And for his own pleasure he felt a desire,*
> *To come to earth and the reason inquire.*
>
> *Well, the lawyer who rose, with a visage so grave,*
> *Made out his opponent a consummate knave;*
> *And Satan felt considerably amused,*
> *To hear the attorney so badly abused.*
>
> *But soon as the speaker had come to a close,*
> *The counsel opposing him fiercely arose,*
> *And heaped such abuse on the head of the first,*
> *That made him a villain of all men the worst.*

Thus they quarreled, contended, and argued so long,
'Twas hard to determine which of them was wrong,
And concluding he'd heard enough of the fuss,
Old Nick turned away, and soliloquized thus:

"They've puzzled the court with their villainous cavil,
And, I'm free to confess it, they've puzzled the Devil;
My agents were right to let lawyers alone,
If I had them they'd swindle me out of my throne."[23]

STRENGTH IN WEAKNESS

Oscar Wilde (1854-1900), Irish poet, dramatist and wit, had a very clear idea of the foibles of the English legal system, but he failed to follow his own advice. He brought about his own downfall when he instituted a libel suit and lost. In happier times, he wrote:

Something may, perhaps be urged on behalf of the Bar.
The mantle of the Sophist has fallen on its members.
Their feigned ardours and unreal rhetoric are
delightful. They can make the worse appear the better
cause . . . and have been known to wrest from reluctant
juries triumphant verdicts of acquittal for their clients,
even when those clients, as often happens, were clearly
and unmistakably innocent.[24]

THE LAWYER AS FIREARM

In *Lord Jeffrey*, published in 1867, the long-lived Thomas Carlyle (1795-1881), wrote:

It is a strange trade, that of advocacy. Your intellect,
your highest heavenly gift, hung up in the shop window
like a loaded pistol for sale, will either blow out a
pestilent scoundrel's brains, or the scoundrel's salutary
sheriff's officer's (in a sense), as you please to choose for
your guinea.[25]

THE LAWYERS EMANCIPATE THE CORPORATIONS

The Fourteenth Amendment to the Constitution, enacted in 1868, forbade the states to ". . . deprive any person of life, liberty or property, without due process of law." The idea behind using "persons" in the Fourteenth Amendment—most of the Constitution refers to "citizens"—was not only to prevent the states from mistreating the newly-freed slaves, but also the millions of immigrants who were pouring into the country. The word "persons" had been used specifically to extend the protection to alien residents. Lawyers for wealthy corporations soon realized, though, that technically a corporation is a "person" in law, *albeit* an artificial person.

In one of the most amazing sleight-of-hand maneuvers ever accomplished by lawyers in the United States, a group of these corporate lawyers convinced the Supreme Court that the Fourteenth Amendment, in referring to "persons," was also designed to protect corporations. Their legal arguments were assisted by the fact that one of the corporate lawyers was former Senator Roscoe Conkling, who helped write the amendment and blithely lied to the court about its framers' intent.

Since then, wealthy corporations have often used their legal status as "just folks" to resist government attempts to improve conditions for workers and to protect consumers. State legislatures soon took the teeth out of this amendment as it applied to the poor and disenfranchised, and lawyers continued to hone it into an ever-more-sophisticated weapon for the rich and powerful.[27]

In 1868, diarist George Templeton Strong (1820-1875), remarked: ***"Bench and Bar settle deeper in the mud every year and every month. They must be near bottom now."***[26]

He was wrong.

"I don't want a lawyer to tell me what I cannot do; I hire him to tell me how to do what I want to do."

J. Pierpont Morgan (1837-1913), American financier[28]

THE PAINLESS PRACTICE OF LAWYER-BASHING

Marshall Brown recounted this anecdote in his *Wit and Humor of Bench and Bar,* not to be confused with his much shorter *Wit and Wisdom of Bench and Bar:*

> *During a trial, counsel, in cross-examining a young physician, made several sarcastic remarks, doubting the ability of so young a man to understand his business. Finally he asked:*
>
> *"Do you know the symptoms of concussion of the brain?"*
>
> *"I do," replied the doctor.*

"Well," continued the attorney, "suppose my learned friend, Mr. Carter, and myself were to bang together, would we get concussion of the brain?"

"Your learned friend, Mr. Carter, might," said the doctor.[29]

A WAY WITH WORDS

Ambrose Bierce (1842-c.1914), author, journalist and professional misanthrope, wrote the *Devil's Dictionary*. In it he concocted the following definitions: "A lawyer: One skilled in the circumvention of the law," "Lawsuit: A machine which you go in as a pig and come out as a sausage," and "Appeal: In law, to put the dice in the box for another throw."

He once related the following anecdote:

A man died leaving a large estate, and many sorrowful relations who claimed it. After some years, when all but one had had judgement given against them, that one was awarded the estate, which he asked his attorney to have appraised.

"There is nothing to appraise," said the attorney, pocketing his last fee.

"Then," said the successful claimant, "what good has all this litigation done me?"

"You have been a good client to me," the attorney replied, gathering up his books and papers. "But I must say you betray a surprising ignorance of the purpose of litigation."[31]

HEADS—I WIN; TAILS—YOU LOSE

The contingent fee, an arrangement under which a lawyer takes as a fee a large percentage of the amount the client is awarded, first became accepted in the United States in the 1840s, but as is shown by this anecdote originally published in the 1880s in the *New York Morning Journal*, it was not well-known even at the end of the century:

A New Yorker asked William Maxwell Evarts what he would charge for managing a certain law case.

"Well," said Mr. Evarts, "I will take your case on a contingent fee."

"And what is a contingent fee?"

"My dear sir," said Mr. Evarts, mellifluously, "I will tell you what a contingent fee to a lawyer means. If I don't win your suit I get nothing. If I do win it you get nothing. See?"[33]

LEGAL LYRICS

Whether you're an honest man or whether you're a thief,
Depends on whose solicitor has given me a brief.

William S. Gilbert (1836-1911),
English dramatist and poet[34]

"Ignorance, superstition, the price of princes, the interest of legislators, caprice, fantasy—these are the sources of the great body of the law."

Anatole France (1844-1924),
French novelist and essayist[35]

JUDGING JUDGES

In an address to the New York Bar Association on January, 17, 1899, Oliver Wendell Holmes, Jr. (1841-1935), had this to say about the bench:

Judges commonly are elderly men, and are more likely to hate at sight any analysis to which they are not accustomed, and which disturbs repose of mind, than to fall in love with novelties.[36]

Robert G. Ingersoll (1833-1899), an American lawyer, politician and orator, made this point about their Honors:

We must remember that we have made judges out of men, and that by being made judges their prejudices are not diminished and their intelligence is not increased.[37]

"A judge is like a carpenter, what he wants, he carves."

Russian Proverb [38]

NOTES

1 Finley Peter Dunne, quoted in Martin Mayer, *The Lawyers*, Harper & Row, New York, 1967, pg. 305.

2 Marshall Brown, *Wit and Humor of Bench and Bar*, George T. Bissel, Philadelphia, 1931, pgs. 146-47.

3 L.J. Bigelow, Bench and Bar: *A Complete Digest of the Wit, Humor, Asperities, and Amenities of the Law*, Harper & Brothers, New York, 1871, pg. 364; J.R. Lewis, *The Victorian Bar*, Robert Hale, London, 1982, pgs. 65-6.

4 Robert Christy, *Proverbs, Maxims and Phrases*, G.P. Putnam's Sons, New York, 1907, pg. 603.

5 Bigelow, *Bench and Bar*, pgs. 445-47.

6 Ralph Warner and Toni Ihara, *29 Reasons Not To Go To Law School*, Nolo Press, Berkeley, 1987, pg. 88.

7 James Hurnard, "The Setting Sun" (1871) from David S. Shrager and Elizabeth Frost, *The Quotable Lawyer*, Facts On File, New York, 1986, pg. 112.

8 Shrager and Frost, *The Quotable Lawyer*, pg. 112.

9 L. Friedman, *Roots of Justice—Crime and Punishment in Alameda County, California,* 1870-1910).

10 Fred and Irwin Silber (eds.), *Folksinger's Wordbook*, Oak Publications, New York, 1973, pg. 34.

11 *New York Times*, September 3, 1902, pg. 9.

12 Richard H. Rovere, *Howe & Hummel: Their True and Scandalous History,* Farrar, Straus and Giroux, New York, 1985, pg. 60.

13 Rovere, *Howe & Hummel, passim.*

14 Herbert V. Prochnow and Herbert V. Prochnow, Jr., *A Treasury of Humorous Quotations*, Harper & Row, New York, 1969, pg. 190.

15 Bigelow, *Bench and Bar*, pg. 326

16 A.K. Adams, *The Home Book of Humorous Quotations*, Harper & Row, New York, 1969, pg. 196.

17 On the Decay of the Art of Lying in Lawrence Teacher (ed.), *The Unabridged Mark Twain*, Running Press, Philadelphia, 1976, pg. 742.

18 Brown, *Wit and Humor of Bench and Bar*, pg. 198.

19 Selwyn G. Champion, *Racial Proverbs: A Selection of the World's Proverbs arranged Linguistically*, Barnes and Noble, New York, 1950, pg. 303.

20 From *Notes and Queries*, Vol. XII (1855), pg. 44 quoted in "Croke," *Lyrics of the Law*, pgs. 123-26.

21 Irving Browne, *Law and Lawyers in Literature*, Soule and
Bugbee, Boston, 1883 (reprinted by Wm. W. Gaunt & Sons,
Inc., Holmes Beach, Florida, 1982), pg. 279.

22 Eli Perkins (ed.), *Wit and Humor of the Age*, Ross Publishing
House, Albany (NY), 1889, pg. 424.

23 From *Western Jurist*, Vol. XV, pg. 287 quoted in "J.
Greenbag Croke," *Lyrics of the Law*, Sumner Whitney & Co.,
San Francisco, 1884 (reprinted by William S. Hein & Co.,
Buffalo, NY, 1986, pgs. 130-31.

24 Oscar Wilde, *The Decay of Lying* (1889) from *The Writings
of Oscar Wilde*, Vol. 10, Keller-Farmer, New York, 1907,
pgs. 10-11.

25 Thomas Carlyle, *Lord Jeffrey* (1867), from H.L. Mencken, *A
New Dictionary of Quotations on Historical Principles*,
Alfred E. Knopf, New York, 1942, pg. 668.

26 George Martin, *Causes and Conflicts: The Centennial History
of the Association of the Bar of the City of New York 1870-
1970*, Houghton Mifflin, Boston, 1970.

27 Mayer, *The Lawyers*, pg. 314.

28 Fred Metcalf, *The Penguin Dictionary of Modern Humorous
Quotations*, Viking, 1986, pg. 146.

29 Marshall Brown, *Wit and Humor of Bench and Bar*, T.H.
Flood & Co., Chicago, 1899 (reprinted by Fred B. Rothman
& Co., Littleton, Colorado, 1986), pg.447.

30 Laurence J. Peter, *Peter's Quotations: Ideas for Our Times*,
William Morrow Co., New York, 1977, pg. 288.

31 Nolo News, Spring, 1985, pg. 20.

32 In *The Kingdom of God is Within You* (1893) from George
Seldes, *The Great Quotations*, Lyle Stuart, New York, 1960,
pg. 688.

33 Perkins, *Wit and Humor of the Age*, pg. 387.

34 William S. Gilbert, *Utopia Limited,* Act I (1893); Mencken,
New Dictionary of Quotations, pg. 668.

35 Rudolph Franz Flesch (ed.), *New Book of Unusual
Quotations*, Harper and Row, New York, 1966.

36 Oliver W. Holmes, *Law in Science, Science in Law*, 1921,
quoted in Schrager and Frost, *The Quotable Lawyer*, pg. 146.

37 Ingersoll, Speech in Washington, DC, October 22, 1883,
quoted in Mencken, *New Dictionary*, pg. 620.

38 Selwyn Gurney Champion, *Racial Proverbs*, Barnes &
Noble, New York, 1950, pg. 263.

CHAPTER SEVEN

FROM
THE TURN OF
THE CENTURY TO
WORLD WAR II

HISTORICAL BRIEF

Great Advancements in the Legal Profession

As the century turned, American lawyers were finding personal injury cases increasingly lucrative. Their usual cut had risen from the 15 to 20 percent common in the Nineteenth Century to 40, 50 and even 60 percent. Still, since the bar association banned advertising by lawyers, they had trouble hooking up with profitable injured parties.

A young man named Abraham Gatner—who interestingly enough, was not a lawyer—solved the problem. In 1907, he persuaded a Manhattan law firm to hire him to track down accident victims. Gatner's method was to go through a list of accidents he received each morning from a police reporter, who was tipped a dollar. To describe this new professional advancement, Gatner coined the term "ambulance chasing." Soon, attorneys started to eliminate the middleperson by working directly with ambulance drivers, hospital attendants and doctors.[1]

The increased use of this arrangement was not universally welcomed. According to Reginald Heber Smith, who wrote the first book criticizing the lack of legal services to the poor around 1917:

> *The contingent fee . . . attracted undesirable persons to become members of the profession. Because the stakes were high and the players essentially gamblers it induced the unholy triumvirate of lawyer-runner-doctor conspiring together to win fraudulent cases. It has degraded expert testimony and served as a cloak for robbery through extortionate fees. Unquestionably, it has done more than anything else to bring the bar into deserved disrepute.[2]*

LEGAL LYRICS

Too Little Known

Carl Sandburg (1878-1967), is one of America's best known poets. This poem, "The Lawyers Know Too Much," published in 1916, was once among his famous works, although today it languishes in undeserved obscurity:

> *The lawyers, Bob, know too much.*
> *They are chums of the books of old John Marshall.*
> *They know it all, what a dead hand wrote,*

A stiff dead hand and its knuckles crumbling,
The bones of the fingers a thin white ash.
The lawyers know a dead man's thoughts too well.
In the heels of the higgling lawyers, Bob,
Too many slippery ifs and buts and howevers,
Too much hereinbefore provided whereas,
Too many doors to go in and out of.

When the lawyers are through
What is there left, Bob?
Can a mouse nibble at it
And find enough to fasten a tooth in?

Why is there always a secret singing
When a lawyer cashes in?
Why does a hearse horse snicker
Hauling a lawyer away?

The work of a bricklayer goes to the blue.
The knack of a mason outlasts a moon.
The hands of a plasterer hold a room together.
The land of a farmer wishes him back again.
Singers of songs and dreamers of plays
Build a house no wind blows over.
The lawyers—tell me why a hearse horse snickers
hauling a lawyer's bones.[3]

PRESIDENTIAL WISDOM

"I used to be a lawyer, but now I am a reformed character."
Woodrow Wilson (1856-1924),
28th President of the United States[4]

HIS DAZE AS A LAWYER

Arthur Train (1875-1945), was a successful lawyer in New York, both in private practice and as Assistant District Attorney from1901 to 1908 and 1914 to 1915. He saw the error of his ways, though, turned to writing, and produced dozens of novels, plays and non-fiction accounts of the law. In this passage from a book entitled *My Day in Court*, Train reminisces about his early days in the business:

> *Another famous legal team was that of O'Hare and*
> *Dineen, for the senior of whom I acquired a genuine*
> *affection. "Steve" O'Hare was a highly cultivated man of*
> *rough exterior, an excellent lawyer, who had been*

educated for the priesthood. His word was as good as, if not better than, his bond.

"Young feller," said O'Hare to me one day, after a jury had gone out, "there's lots of things in this game you ain't got onto yet. Do you think I care what the jury did? Not a mite. I got a nice little error into this case the very first day, and I've set back ever since. S'pose we are convicted? I'll get Jim here out on a certificate of reasonable doubt and it'll be two whole years before the Court of Appeals will get around to the case. Meantime Jim'll be out makin' money to pay me my fee—won't you Jim? Then your witnesses will all be gone, and nobody'll remember what on earth it was all about. You'll be down on Wall Street practicing real law yourself, and the indictment'll kick around the office for a year or so, all covered with dust, and then some day I'll get a friend of mine to come in quietly and move to dismiss. And it'll be dismissed! Don't you worry! Why, a thousand other murders will have been committed in this country by the time that happens. Bless your soul! You can't go on tryin' the same man forever. Give the other fellers a chance! You shake your head? Well, it's a fact! I've been doin' it for thirty years. You'll see!"

And—before I got through—I saw.[5]

INJUSTICE FOR ALL

Jean Giradeaux (1882-1944), the French diplomat, novelist and playwright, had an artistic view of the legal profession:

There's no better way of exercising the imagination than the study of law. No poet ever interpreted nature as freely as a lawyer interprets truth.[6]

In *The Madwoman of Chaillot,* written a year before his death, one of his characters says:

You're an attorney. It's your duty to lie, conceal and distort everything and slander everybody.[7]

COURTROOM DRAMATICS

Finley Peter Dunne (1867-1936), spent the first quarter of this century sending up America's establishment in the person of his philosophical alter-ego Mr. Dooley. In the following selection, Dooley laments the metamorphosis of the lawyer from

an orator into an operator. It is clear that he prefers a gasbag to
a moneybag:

*D'ye raymember Grogan? He was me lawyer in thim
days. Whin I had wrongs that I didn't propose to have
trampled on, I took thim to Grogan, an' Grogan
presinted thim to th' coort. Deat me, but 'twas a threet to
see an' hear him. He'd been a pedlar in his youth, an'
ye cud hear his voice as far as th' Indyanny State line.
Whin he talked to th' judge ye'd think he was hollerin'
insthructions to a ship-wrecked sailor against th' wind. I
can see him now as he knelt on th' flure an' called
Heaven to witnes th' justice iv his cause, or stalked
acrost th' room to where me opponent sat an' hissed in
his ear, "Polthroon." Whin he spoke iv th' other lawyer
as "me larned Brother" he done it is such a way that ye
expect th' other lawyer to reach f'r a gun.*

*An it wasn't all talkin' ayether. 'Twas th' hardest kind iv
exercise. His arms were always in motion. He wud bate
th' table with his fist till th' coort house thrembled. He
wud shake his head till ye'd think he'd shake it off. If he
was th' lawyer in a case of assault an' batthry he'd
punch himself in th' jaw an' fall over a chair to show th'
jury how it happened. If 'twas a murdher thrile he'd
pretind to shoot himself through th' heart an' sink to th'
ground dead with his head in a wastepaper basket an'
his foot in a juryman's lap. If 'twas a breach iv promise
suit he'd kneel on th' flure in front iv a juryman that
looked soft an' beg him to be his. There was no kind iv
acrobat that ye iver see in a circus that cud give
annything to Grogan. An' whin he'd filled th' air with
beautiful language an' baten th' coort room furniture
into slivers, he'd sink down in his chair overcome be his
emotions, with th' tears pourin' fr'm his eyes, an' give ye
th' wink fr'm behind his han'derchief.*[8]

Dooley also wrote:

*Don't I think a poor man has a chanst in court? Iv
coorse he has. He has the same chanst there that he has
outside. He has a splendid poor man's chanst.*[9]

ROGUES GALLERY

William Fallon (1886-1927)

Oliver Wendell
Holmes, Jr.
(1841-1935),
Associate Justice of
the Supreme Court
from 1902 to 1932,
once reprimanded
a youthful lawyer
for his
overenthusiasm.
Said the Justice:

*"This is a court
of law, young
man, not a court
of justice."*[10]

The term "mouthpiece" originated around 1910 as a New York underworld label for the criminal lawyer who made a shady living defending crooks and gangsters. Although these lawyers kept them out of jail, the pimps, bootleggers and killers of New York had little respect for their defenders, and the term is one of derision. Underworld lawyers proliferated, but only one was universally known and appreciated as The Great Mouthpiece: William Fallon.

Fallon was in turn flamboyant, insulting, brilliant, crooked and drunk. During the years 1918 to 1924, practicing from a humble office in Times Square, he was one of the best-known criminal lawyers in the city and certainly the shadiest. Between his late-night jaunts to the theaters and night clubs, his drunken jags and his trysts, he packed in an impressive quantity, if not quality, of lawyering. He defended gambler and former lightweight boxing champion Abe Attell in the Black Sox Scandal—saving him by bribing a gambler who had lost money by betting on the Sox into recanting his earlier identification of Attell as a fixer. He worked for Dandy Phil Kastel, a tireless con man of the day, and Nicky Arnstein, another charming con man once married to actress Fannie Brice. He was the lawyer for Arnold Rothstein, called "The Big Bankroll" and "Mr. Big," the kingpin of the New York underworld. He defended hundreds of petty criminals, bootleggers and con artists. But Fallon had his principles: He would not take on actions for divorce. He declared piously: "I am fundamentally opposed to divorce because of religious grounds and my own personal taste."

But his religious principles covered little other territory. A typical Fallon story goes like this: A terrified bank teller once called on him in a panic. The man had embezzled $10,000 and lost it all gambling. The bank examiners were hot on his trail. He faced certain ruin; his family certain shame.

"How much more can you get?" asked Fallon.

The teller was nonplussed. He had come to get out of his scrape, not to enlarge it.

Fallon persisted: "Could you get $50,000 and be back here with it before the examiners get there?"

Still puzzled, the teller admitted that he could, and Fallon had him return the next day with fifty thousand and then registered the man in a hotel under an assumed name. Fallon then called the bank president.

"You're $50,000 short in your accounts," he informed the banker. "I represent the teller who took the money. I think I can recover forty thousand of it if you agree not to prosecute."

The banker, outraged at first, eventually agreed to the deal to recoup as much money as possible and avoid publicity. Fallon returned forty thousand and pocketed the rest.[11]

Fallon was a dramatic courtroom orator—eloquent and reckless, adept at playing on the sympathies of a jury, casting doubt on the most innocuous testimony, impugning the most innocent witnesses. But to accomplish all this, he relied little on the law. He could browbeat witnesses along with the best, but he took greater delight in the challenge of more creative courtroom tactics. He once completely altered the appearance of a client—putting him on a crash diet, dyeing his hair and giving him a pair of exceedingly thick but completely useless eyeglasses to wear. Unidentified by witnesses, he was acquitted. In another case, Fallon faked rheumatism to play on the sympathies of a similarly afflicted juror. And he pretended during another trial to have a hearing infection so that he could shout at point-blank range in the faces of opposing witnesses.

Others among his tactics were not so original or amusing. He was the counsel in a large number of cases where important documents mysteriously disappeared. And he was counsel in a suspiciously—incredibly, said one biographer—large number of cases that ended, eleven-to-one, in hung juries. It was this odd and recurring combination that led to Fallon's downfall.

Rumors about jury-fixing had circulated for many years, but it was not until May of 1924 that reporters for the *New York American* dug up a juror who confessed to taking a bribe from Fallon. Faced with an indictment, Fallon quickly went into hiding. Fished out of a girlfriend's apartment after three weeks, he turned the tables on his accusers at his trial. Fallon alleged a retaliatory conspiracy by the publisher of the *American*, William Randolph Hearst, claiming he had unearthed one of Hearst's deepest and darkest secrets. He argued that the charges were trumped up to squelch evidence of Hearst's extramarital paternity. "I have here in court," Fallon solemnly intoned, pressing his hand to his breast pocket, "the actual birth certificates of the illegitimate children of a certain motion picture actress!" Whether he actually had the goods—he never pulled a single thing out of his pocket—the strategy worked, and the jury acquitted Fallon. As he left the courtroom, he paused next to *American* reporter Nat Ferber. "Nat," he said, "I promise you I'll never bribe another juror!"

Soon after, Fallon faced disbarment proceedings on numerous charges of misconduct and conflict of interest. An appellate court ruled that Fallon had violated none of the ethics of his profession and dismissed the charges—which says a great deal more about legal ethics than it does about the obviously crooked Fallon.

But he never recovered from the two trials. Business dropped off sharply, his heavy drinking became heavier, his health declined. Fallon died of a gastric hemorrhage, exacerbated by drinking, on April 29, 1927.[12]

JUSTICE IS BLIND—
EXCEPT ON THE POCKET SIDE

To prevent judicial salaries from being used as tools for political pressure, the U.S. Constitution states that a judge's pay cannot be reduced during tenure in office. When the federal government implemented income tax, authorized by the Sixteenth Amendment, some federal judges sued to enjoin the government from collecting the tax on them, on the grounds it would reduce their salaries. Remarkably enough, in 1920, the U.S. Supreme Court Justices, whose own pocketbooks stood to benefit, upheld this self-serving argument. This embarrassing decision was not overruled until 1939.[13]

FREEDOM ISN'T FREE

During a lifetime spent defending the powerless, oppressed and unpopular, Clarence Darrow (1857-1938), gained first-hand knowledge of the difference between the law's image and reality:

> What is "legal freedom?" Everybody always had "legal freedom." The men who were roasted to death by the Spanish Inquisition had "legal freedom." That is, they had all the freedom that the law gave them. The old men and women of America who were hung for witchcraft enjoyed "legal freedom." No man who ever knew the meaning of that word "freedom" ever attached to it the word "legal."[14]

A FEE BY ANY OTHER NAME

Alfred E. Smith (1873-1944), was governor of New York twice—from 1919 to 1920 and from 1923 to1928. As this anecdote from Robert Caro's *The Power Broker* indicates, Smith was not fond of lawyers:

> Strolling through a law school library one day, the Governor noticed a student poring intently over his books. "There," he said,

with a smile, "is a young man studying how to take a bribe and call it a fee."15

THE SCANDAL SHEET

Teapot Dome

Next to Watergate, the Teapot Dome Scandal of the Harding Administration is the best-known saga of American political corruption and greed. It centered around the Department of the Interior, which leased federal oil reserves to private companies. For these lucrative contracts, Edward Doheny of the Pan-American Petroleum and Transport Company, and Harry F. Sinclair, of the Mammoth Oil Company, kicked back bonds and cash worth nearly $400,000 to their old friend, who happened to be Secretary of the Interior. That friend was Albert B. Fall, attorney at law. On July 18, 1931, after being convicted of conspiracy to defraud the government, Fall became the first Cabinet officer in American history to go to prison. He served a year in the New Mexico State Penitentiary, and died in 1944.17

"The minute you read something you don't understand, you can be almost sure it was drawn up by a lawyer."

Will Rogers (1879-1935), American actor and humorist16

ANOTHER MODEST PROPOSAL

H.L. Mencken (1880-1956), noted American journalist, lexicographer and cynic, revealed his attitude toward the legal profession with his definition:

Lawyer: One who protects us against robbers by taking away the temptation.

Of the bench he wrote:

The penalty for laughing in the courtroom is six months in jail: if it were not for this penalty, the jury would never hear the evidence.

And he once described a courtroom as:

A place where Jesus Christ and Judas Iscariot would be equals, with the betting odds in favor of Judas.18

In 1924, Mencken mused in the *Baltimore Evening Sun:*

All the extravagance and incompetence of our present government is due in the main to lawyers. They are responsible for nine-tenths of the useless and vicious laws that clutter the statute books and for all the evils that go with the vain attempt to enforce them. Every federal judge is a lawyer. So are most congressmen. Every invasion of the plain rights of the citizen has a lawyer behind it. If all lawyers were hanged tomorrow, and their bones sold to a mah jong factory, we would be freer and safer and our taxes would be reduced by almost one-half.[19]

THE EVER-WAXING BAR

In 1900, California had 4,000 lawyers. Less than three decades later, the number had doubled. In 1928, Dean Marion R. Kirkwood of Stanford Law School complained in the *California State Bar Journal* about the explosion in the number of lawyers in the state:

> *We have more lawyers today than there is any legitimate need for . . . The truth is that we are simply being swamped with aspiring young lawyers, most of whom will necessarily and within a few years after admission drift into real estate, insurance and related lines, and that is not a process calculated to help the reputation of our profession.*[20]

In the six decades since Kirkwood wrote, the number of lawyers in California has reached 120,000—an increase of 1,500%.

LONGEVITY SANS INTEGRITY

In 1935, the University of Pennsylvania conferred the degree of Doctor of Laws upon Alfred Edward Newton, the English wit and writer. This is a selection from his speech on that occasion, which was entitled *Newton on Blackstone:*

> *How favorably situated is the lawyer compared with the physician! A physician has a rich patient who is taken ill; the physician makes a grievous mistake in his diagnosis, the patient dies, and his colleague, the undertaker, comes into his own. With the lawyer it is not so. When he makes a mistake he asks for a "refresher," as fees were formerly called, demands a new trial, and so proceeds **ad infinitum.** For the law is not an exact science like mathematics, which is above all things monotonous....When lawyers multiply they multiply words, and no one can foretell what the result may be....You cannot have failed to observe, sir, the extreme age to which lawyers live. Age does not wither them, nor does custom stale. This is for the reason that they have no cares or anxieties of their own; the cares and anxieties of their clients touch them only as the sun*

"The law is simply and solely made for the exploitation of those who do not understand it or those who, for naked need, cannot obey it."

Bertolt Brecht (1898-1956), German playwright[21]

*touches the flower: it causes them to blossom like a
rose....*[22]

THE LABYRINTH OF LEGAL LANGUAGE

One of the first and best of the modern era's anti-lawyer
books is *Woe Unto You, Lawyers!* written in 1939 by lawyer and
Yale law professor Fred Rodell (1907-). In a chapter entitled
"More About Legal Language," Rodell explains that the purpose
of language is not always to communicate:

> . . . *Almost all legal sentences, whether they appear in
> judges' opinions, written statutes or ordinary bills of
> sale, have a way of reading as though they had been
> translated from the German by someone with a rather
> meager knowledge of English. Invariably they are long.
> Invariably they are awkward. Invariably and inevitably
> they make plentiful use of the abstract, fuzzy, clumsy
> words which are so essential to the solemn hocus-pocus
> of the Law.*

> *Now it is generally conceded that the purpose of
> language, whether written, spoken, or gestured, is that
> which conveys ideas from one person to another. The
> best kind of language, the best use of language, is that
> which conveys ideas most clearly and most completely . .
> . But the language of the Law seems almost deliberately
> designed to confuse and muddle the ideas it purports to
> convey. That quality of legal language can itself only be
> useful on only one supposition. It can be useful only if
> the ideas themselves are so confused and muddled and
> empty that an attempt to express those ideas in clear
> precise language would betray their true nature. In that
> case muddiness of expression can serve very nicely to
> conceal muddiness of thought. And no segment of the
> English language in use today is so muddy, so con-
> fusing, so hard to pin down to its supposed meaning, as
> the language of the Law. It ranges only from the
> ambiguous to the completely incomprehensible.*[24]

**"Litigation: A form
of hell whereby
money is
transferred from the
pockets of the
proletariat to that of
lawyers."**

Frank McKinney Hubbard
(1868-1930), author and
journalist[23]

**"Virtue in the
middle," said the
Devil, as he sat
down between two
lawyers.**

Danish Proverb[25]

SELECTIONS FROM A MASTER

Franz Kafka (1883-1924)

Kafka studied law from 1901 to 1906, where he no doubt sharpened his sense of the absurd. Although he obtained his law degree, he only practiced one year, spending the bulk of his career as an insurance executive. In his novel *The Trial,* and in several of his short stories, Kafka dealt with the law, finding its everyday enigmas, perplexities and randomness ideal for his bizarre brand of treatment.

The Trial

Joseph K., arrested "one morning, without his having done anything wrong," pays a visit to his lawyer to find out something about his mystifying case. All he gets is more mystification:

[His lawyer] had already, so he would relate, won many similar cases either outright or partially. Cases which, though in reality not quite so difficult, perhaps, as this one, had been outwardly still more hopeless. He had a list of these cases in a drawer of his desk—at this he tapped one of them—but he regretted he couldn't show it, as it was a matter of official secrecy. Nevertheless the vast experience he had gained through all these cases would now redound to K.'s benefit. He had started on K.'s case at once, of course, and the first plea was almost ready for presentation. That was very important, for the first impression made by the Defense often determined the whole course of subsequent proceedings.

Though, unfortunately, it was his duty to warn K., it sometimes happened that the first pleas were not read by the Court at all. They simply filed them among the other papers and pointed out that for the time being the observation and interrogation of the accused were more important than any formal petition. If the petitioner pressed them, they generally added that before the verdict was pronounced all the material accumulated, including, of course, every document relating to the case, the first plea as well, would be carefully examined. But unluckily even that was not quite true in most cases, the first plea was often mislaid or lost altogether and, even if it were kept intact till the end, was hardly ever read; that was of course, the lawyer admitted, merely a rumor.[26]

Before the Law

The following is a short parable, published by Kafka in 1916, presented in its entirety:

Before the Law stands a doorkeeper. To this doorkeeper there comes a man from the country and prays for admittance to the Law. But the doorkeeper says that he cannot grant admittance at the moment. The man thinks it over and then asks if he will be allowed in later. "It is possible," says the doorkeeper, "but not at the moment." Since the gate stands open, as usual, and the doorkeeper steps to one side, the man stoops to peer through the gateway into the interior. Observing that, the doorkeeper laughs and says: "If you are so drawn to it, just try to go in despite my veto. But take note: I am powerful. And I am only the least of the doorkeepers. From hall to hall there is one doorkeeper after another, each more powerful than the last. The third doorkeeper is already so terrible that even I cannot bear to look at him." These are difficulties the man from the country has not expected; the Law, he thinks, should surely be accessible at all times and to everyone, but as he now takes a close look at the doorkeeper in his fur coat, with his big sharp nose and long, thin, black Tartar beard, he decides that it is better to wait until he gets permission to enter. The doorkeeper gives him a stool and lets him sit down at one side of the door. There he sits for days and years. He makes many attempts to be admitted, and wearies the doorkeeper by his importunity. The doorkeeper frequently has little interviews with him, asking him questions about his home and many other things, but the questions are put indifferently, as great lords put them, and always finish with the statement that he cannot be let in yet. The man, who has furnished himself with many things for his journey, sacrifices all he has, however valuable, to bribe the doorkeeper. The doorkeeper accepts everything, but always with the remark: "I am only taking it to keep you from thinking you have omitted anything." During these many years the man fixes his attention almost continuously on the doorkeeper. He forgets the other doorkeepers, and this first one seems to him the sole obstacle preventing access to the Law. He curses his bad luck, in his early years boldly and loudly; later, as he grows old, he only grumbles to himself. He becomes childish, and since in his yearlong contemplation of the doorkeeper he has come to know even the fleas in his fur collar, he begs the fleas as well to help him and to change the doorkeeper's mind. At length his eyesight begins to fail, and he does not know whether the world is really darker or whether his eyes are only deceiving him. Yet in his

darkness he is now aware of a radiance that streams inextinguishably from the gateway of the Law. Now he has not very long to live. Before he dies, all his experiences in these long years gather themselves in his head to one point, a question he had not yet asked the doorkeeper. He waves him nearer, since he can no longer raise his stiffening body. The doorkeeper has to bend low toward him, for the difference in height between them has altered much to the man's disadvantage. "What do you want to know now?" asks the doorkeeper; "you are insatiable." "Everyone strives to reach the Law," says the man, "so how does it happen that for all these many years no one but myself has ever begged for admittance?" The doorkeeper recognizes that the man has reached his end, and, to let his failing senses catch the words, roars in his ear: "No one else could ever be admitted here, since this gate was made only for you. I am now going to shut it." [27]

The Advocates

This selection is from a short, dreamlike story never published in Kafka's lifetime. Perhaps he feared a lawsuit:

I could not even find out whether we were in a law court. Some facts spoke for it, others against. What reminded me of a law court more than all the details was a droning noise which could be heard incessantly in the distance; one could not tell from which direction it came, it filled every room to such an extent that one had to assume it came from everywhere, or, what seemed more likely, that just the place where one happened to be standing was the very place where the droning originated, but this was probably an illusion, for it came from a distance. These corridors, narrow and austerely vaulted, turning in gradual curves with high, sparsely decorated doors, seemed to have been created specially for profound silence; they were the corridors of a museum or a library. Yet if it were not a law court, why was I searching for an advocate here? Because I was searching for an advocate everywhere; he is needed everywhere, if anything less in court than elsewhere, for a court, one assumes, passes judgment according to the law. If one were to assume that this was being done unfairly or frivolously, then life would not be possible; one must have confidence that the court allows the majesty of the law its full scope, for this is its sole duty. Within the law all is accusation, advocacy, and verdict; any interference by an individual here would be a crime. It is different however, in the case of the verdict itself; this is based on inquiries being made here and there, from relatives and strangers, from friends and enemies, in the family and public life, in town and village—in short, everywhere. Here it is most necessary to have advocates, one next to the other, a living wall, for advocates are by nature hard to set in motion; the plaintiffs, however, those sly foxes, those slinking weasels, those little mice, they slip through the tiniest gaps, scuttle through the legs of the advocates. So look out! That's why I am here, I'm collecting advocates.[28]

THAT GOES DOUBLE FOR YOU

F.E. Smith, the first Earl of Birkenhead (1872-1930), was for many years a star of the Australian bar. His lack of respect for the bench was proverbial:

Judge: *"You are offensive, Sir."*

Smith: *"We both are; the difference is that I'm trying to be and you can't help it."*[29]

SEE NO EVIL?

As part of a general critique of the adversarial process, Franklin D. Stier, a law professor at the California State University at Dominguez Hills, describes the following travesty of justice:

The controversial Charlie Chaplin paternity suit in 1943 illustrates the persuasive power of attorney guile. Conclusive scientific evidence—a blood test—refuted the plaintiff's claim that Chaplin had fathered her child. Even so, the plaintiff prevailed due to a masterful appeal to the emotions of the jurors by her attorney. He portrayed Chaplin as the wealthy villain, callously indifferent to the consequences of his alleged indiscretions. His presentation featured a dramatic juxtaposition of the infant's face next to Chaplin's so that the jury could "see" the physical similarities. Later, he climactically shed tears over the plight of his destitute client and her child. A professional courtroom actor thus bested one of the foremost film actors of all time. We can only speculate whether the irony was lost on Chaplin.[30]

IF PROCEDURE IS RIGHT,
I DON'T WANNA BE WRONGED

There is no reason why a plain, honest man should not be permitted to go into court and tell his story and have

*the judge before whom he comes permitted to do justice
in that particular case, unhampered by a great variety
of statutory rules . . . We have got our procedure regulated according to the trained, refined, subtle, ingenious
intellect of the best practiced lawyers, and it is all
wrong.*

Elihu Root (1845-1937), Secretary of State and
Nobel Peace Prize winner[31]

THE EMANCIPATION DISSIMULATION

Since its inception, the American Bar Association has
worked hard and successfully to make the practice of law a
monopoly—open only to those who are accredited by state
bars. It has been argued by legal reform groups that lawyers be
compelled to do *pro bono* work on behalf of the
underrepresented poor. Lawyers claim that this would violate
the Thirteenth Amendment, which emancipated the slaves,
claiming that being compelled to do free legal work for the poor
represents involuntary servitude.

*For the men of law are a monopoly, and monopoly is
subject to regulation. The ground for monopoly is that it
makes possible better service; this holds of the bar. The
condition of monopoly is that it serve; this does not hold
of the bar. If it were gas or transportation these men of
law were furnishing, the established policy and rule
would be service to all comers on demand and no
refusal, at fixed and reasonable rates, by state com-
pulsion. The bar, man by man or firm by firm, set their
own fees, choose among clients, and leave the bulk of
needed service unperformed—the poor man's case.*

*Law is a profession in theory, and a monopoly in fact; a
monopoly not merely by force of skill and brain but
established and maintained by law. Only through
lawyers can the layman win in fact the rights the law
purports to give him.*

Karl N. Llewellyn (1893-1962),
American law professor[32]

TAKE MY ADVICE . . . PLEASE

Sir Patrick Hastings (1880-1952), was the Attorney-General
in the United Kingdom under Ramsey MacDonald in the early
1930s, and in addition, wrote several books and plays. Only a

few months after representing a defendant, he found himself cross-examining the very same man in another trial. Sir Patrick, who had no recollection of their former relationship, warned the witness:

"You will answer my questions directly, take my advice."

"I will not take your advice sir," replied the witness. "I took it once and it put me inside for six months."[33]

COMMENCING TO INCORPORATE

This historical period saw an ever-larger number of lawyers turning from advocacy of the individual to employment by Big Business. Supreme Court Justice Harlan F. Stone (1872-1946), commented acerbically on the explosive growth in corporate law—and its attendant corporate servitude—during a commencement speech at the University of Michigan in June of 1934:

> *The successful lawyer of our day more often than not is the proprietor or general manager of a new type of factory, whose legal product is increasingly the result of mass production methods. More and more the amount of his income is the measure of professional success. More and more he must look for his rewards to the material satisfactions derived from profits as from a successfully conducted business, rather than to the intangible and indubitably more durable satisfactions which are to be found in a professional service more consciously directed toward the advancement of the public interest. Steadily the best skill and capacity of the profession has been drawn into the exacting and highly specialized service of business and finance. At its best the changed system has brought to the command of the business world loyalty and a superb proficiency and technical skill. At its worst it has made the learned profession of an earlier day the obsequious servant of business, and tainted it with the morals and manners of the market place in its most anti-social manifestations.*[34]

The Association of the Bar of New York City did not admit women until 1937.[35]

NAZI LAWYERS, NAZI JUDGES

In 1944, General de Baer, the Belgian representative to the United Nations War Crimes Commission, wrote in a secret report:

> *It seems that hitherto the National [War Crimes] Offices have restricted themselves to sending us only "crimes" in the popular conception of that word, and the consequence is that . . . the person in whom the crime really*

originated is not mentioned. We are referring specially to those German lawyers who, in the tranquillity of their study, have conceived those measures which have afforded others the possibility to unleash their savage instincts with impunity and covered in advance those unspeakable acts under a cloak of legality.[36]

In addition to setting up the legal structure for Nazi crimes, German and Austrian lawyers and judges participated enthusiatically in the judicial tortures and murders perpetrated under the Third Reich. Over 45,000 death sentences were handed out in twelve years—the vast majority for traditionally non-capital offenses, such as theft; petty crimes, such as black-out violations; and many for "racial" crimes, such as sexual relations between Jews and Christians. One judge sentenced a Jewish man to death for kissing an employee on the cheek.

After the war, not a single judge was tried for judicial murder. Even more amazingly, the entire National Socialist legal system was left intact by the British, French and American occupiers. Only one judge was removed—by the French. Not a single lawyer was disbarred because of a Nazi past. And the legal decisions of Nazi courts are still respected under German law today.[37]

NOTES

1   Martin Mayer, *The Lawyers*, Harper & Row, New York, 1967, pg 260.

2   Mayer, *The Lawyers*, pgs. 260-61; Reginald Heber Smith, *Justice and the Poor,* Arno Press, New York, 1971 (originally published 1917), pg. 86.

3   Carl Sandburg, "The Lawyers Know Too Much" (1916) from *The Complete Poems of Carl Sandburg*, Harcourt Brace Jovanovich, New York, 1970, pg. 189.

4   Evan Esar, *20,000 Quips and Quotes*, Doubleday & Co., Garden City, NY, 1968, pg. 464.

5   Arthur Train, *My Day in Court*, Charles Scribners' Sons, New York, 1939, pgs. 30-31.

6   Jean Giradeaux, *Tiger at the Gates* (1935), 2, from Tripp, *International Thesaurus of Quotations*, Thomas Y. Crowell Co., New York, 1970, pg. 344. Translated by Christopher Fry.

7   Jean Giradeaux, *Madwoman of Chaillot* (1945), 2, from Rhoda T. Tripp (ed.), *International Thesaurus of Quotations*, pg. 344. Translated by Maurice Valency.

8   "Mr. Dooley on Lawyer"s, by Finley Peter Dunne, from *The Speaker,* 1905, in William Lloyd Prosser, *The Judicial Humorist*, Little, Brown and Co., Boston, 1952.

9   Mayer, *The Lawyers*, pg. 272; Bander (ed.), *Mr. Dooley on the Choice of Law,* pgs. xxii-xxiii.

10   Laurence J. Peter, *Peter's Quotations: Ideas for Our Times*, William Morrow Co., New York, 1977, pg. 276.

11   Alan Hynd, *Defenders of the Damned*, A.S. Barnes & Co., New York, 1960, pgs. 123-25.

12   Hynd, *Defenders of the Damned*, passim; Gene Fowler, *The Great Mouthpiece: A Life Story of William J. Fallon*, Covici, Friede, 1931, passim.

13   Mayer, *The Lawyers*, pg. 502.

14   Clarence Darrow: *Attorney for the Damned*, Arthur Weinberg (ed.), Simon and Schuster, New York, 1957.

15   R. Caro, *The Power Broker*, Random House, New York, 1975, pg. 713.

16   Peter, *Peter's Quotations*, pg. 293.

17   Nathan Miller, *The Founding Finaglers*, David McKay Co., Inc., New York, 1976, pgs. 317-49.

18   Peter, *Peter's Quotations*, pg. 288.

19   Quoted by V. Corsetti, *Nolo News*, Spring, 1987, pg. 11.

20 "Too Many Lawyers," *Americans for Legal Reform*, April/June, Vol. 8, No. 3, pg. 32.

21 Bertold Brecht, *Three Penny Opera* 3.1 from Tripp (ed.), *International Thesaurus of Quotations*, pg. 343.

22 Alfred E. Newton, *Newton on Blackstone*, University of Pennsylvania Press, Philadelphia, 1937.

23 Frank McKinney Hubbard, The Roycroft Dictionary and Book of Epigrams, (1923) quoted in David S. Shrager and Elizabeth Frost, *The Quotable Lawyer*, Facts On File, New York, 1986, pg. 122.

24 Fred Rodell, *Woe Unto You, Lawyers!*, Pageant Press, New York, 1957 (reprinted by Fred. B. Rothman & Co., Littleton, Colorado, 1987), pgs. 124-25.

25 H.L. Mencken, *A New Dictionary of Quotations on Historical Principles*, Alfred E. Knopf, New York, 1942, pg. 668.

26 Franz Kafka, *The Trial*, Alfred A. Knopf, New York, 1956, pgs. 143-44. Translated by Willa and Edwin Muir.

27 Franz Kafka, "Before the Law" in *Franz Kafka: The Complete Stories*, Nahum N. Glatzer (ed.), Schocken Books, New York, 1983, pgs. 3-4.

28 Franz Kafka "Advocates" in Glatzer (ed.), *Franz Kafka: The Complete Stories,* pgs. 449- 50.

29 F.E. Smith, 2nd Earl of Birkenhead, *Legal Litter*, Caxton Press, Christchurch, New Zealand, 1977, pg. 39.

30 Franklin Delano Stier, "The Real Crisis in the Courts," *The Humanist*, March/April, 1988, pg. 6.

31 Mayer, *The Lawyers*, pg. 276.

32 Karl N. Llewellyn quoted in Ralph Nader and Mark Green (eds.), *Verdicts on Lawyers*, Thomas Y. Crowell Co., New York, 1976, pg. ix.

33 Gary Alderdice, *First Thing We Do...Let's Kill All The Lawyers*, privately printed, Hong Kong, 1984, pg. 6.

34 Mayer, *The Lawyers* pg. 339; Harlan F. Stone, "The Public Influence of the Bar" 48 Harvard Law Review 1 pgs. 6-7.

35 George Whitney Martin, *Causes and Conflict*, Houghton Mifflin, Boston, 1970, pgs. 244-45.

36 General de Baer, *Report to the United Nations War Crimes Commission*, May 2, 1944, UNWCC Archives, Reel 33, Document M.16.

37 Tom Bower, *Blind Eye to Murder*, Andre Deutsch, London, 1981 pgs. 190-96.

CHAPTER EIGHT

FROM
WORLD WAR II
TO THE PRESENT

HISTORICAL BRIEF

The Briefly Popular Lawyer

The 1940s through the '60s were extraordinarily successful years for the legal profession. In stature, in income and in numbers, lawyers did increasingly well. Indeed, it was something of a Golden Age for the bar—a time when an attorney could be admired for a razor-sharp intellect, faultless deduction and professionalism, as well as for being a member of the best country club. Many parents actually wanted their children to grow up to be attorneys.

The boom times in the economy generally were a big reason behind the good times for lawyers. America's worldwide business hegemony gave attorneys steady and increasingly lucrative work in the corporate sphere. At the same time, the burgeoning middle class, a group always respectful of professionals, put more new money in their pockets. And best of all, these newfound riches all went to a relatively few lawyers—the Depression and Second World War having limited the flow of young men into law schools.

The profession also gained respect for its courtroom victories in the civil rights struggle. The noble battles of lawyers like Thurgood Marshall, Leonard Boudin, William Kunstler and Vincent Hallinan in desegregating schools, buses, restaurants and other public facilities turned them into something of folk heroes. It also created role models that many a youth tried to emulate by naively enrolling in law school, hoping to learn how to do good while at the same time doing very well.

And finally, there is little doubt that the indomitable and unerring Perry Mason, crusading through his television courtroom while barking orders at the ever-patient and respectful Della Street from 1957 until 1966, had a substantial effect in enhancing the reputation of the profession.

But while it was a Golden Age for many lawyers, not everyone was taken in by the glitter. By the late '60s, a public backlash had begun. To a great extent, lawyers were victims of their own success. They began to make too much money, pricing themselves beyond the reach of their greatest boosters—the middle class—and providing little or no service to the working class or poor. Although most trial lawyers believed, and many still believe, that they stood shoulder to shoulder with their victimized clients against the big guys and fat cats, most people began to see lawyers as big guys and fat cats themselves.

"Those lawyers with Hah-vud accents are always thinking up new ways to take advantage of people."

Harry Truman
(1884-1972),
Thirty-third President of
the United States[1]

LEGAL LYRICS

Raising Kane

In an address before the Missouri Bar Association given in 1947, Dr. R. Emmett Kane remarked: "It is difficult to be kind or even charitable in judging law and lawyers since they are the authors of all the troubles that plague the human race, and have been since time began." He ended his address with the following doggerel, entitled *The Bench and Bar:*

If you've got a son or daughter
Who ain't livin' like they orter,
If they'd suck an egg and peddle you the shell;
If the neighbors and the preacher,
The policeman and the teacher,
Are convinced that they are headed straight for hell;
If their instincts are possessive
And their ego is excessive,
If they're short on brains but very long on jaw,
Don't sit up nights and worry,
Make your mind up in a hurry,
Chuck 'em off to school and make 'em study law.
Have 'em learn the art of stalling,
How to howl like Virtue bawling,
And to make their betters think that they are tops;
How to wheedle fortunes stealthy
From a clientele that's wealthy,
And to be elected judge in case they're flops.
To become a politician
Must, of course, be their ambition,
Help 'em buy all the ghosts they can afford.
It's a lawyer's bounden duty
Be he moron, shyster, cootie,
When the gravy train is moving, be aboard.
He, of course, must hold his licker,
Be a Latin-spouting slicker,
Fill the human race with wholesome fear and awe,
For the life of Riley waits him
Till the Devil ups and dates him
When He's finished with the practice of the Law.

IT TAKES ONE TO KNOW ONE

Willie Sutton (1901-1980), was a sharp, witty and successful bank robber who made the FBI's Most Wanted List in 1951. As he relates in his autobiography, *Where the Money Was*, he had the opportunity to observe both sides of the legal coin. He once considered a career as a lawyer, but decided he could get the same results without wasting three years in law school:

The line between a bank robber and a lawyer is a very thin one, anyway. In robbing a bank I always planned the job carefully, leaving nothing to chance. It's the same thing in trying a case. "Preparation is everything," lawyers say. Once you're inside the bank, you have to see everything, guard yourself against everybody. While he is putting in his case, the lawyer has to be equally alert, equally on guard against anything the other side might throw at him. In both professions, it helps to be a little paranoid.

And whatever they might say in the law schools, it also helps to have a grudge against society. The criminal attacks society head on; the lawyer is trying to set you free after you have been caught so that you can go out and steal some more. Whether he succeeds or not, he profits from your crime. The only way you can pay him is out of the money you have got away with at one time or another, everybody knows that. It isn't called his share of the loot, of course. It's called "the fee." But that's only because he has a license that entitles him to do what he's doing, and you haven't.[3]

CINEMA VERITÉ

Lawyers have always been concerned about their bad image—much more so, in fact, than about the reasons why they are so disliked and distrusted. Lawyers are quick to complain when they feel slighted, not considering that things could be worse, as this story told by columnist and television commentator Andy Rooney (1919-) indicates:

When I was at MGM years ago, I worked for a producer named Voldemar Vetluguin. I was in his office one day when his assistant came in.

"You got an angry letter from the American Bar Association," the assistant said. "They've been keeping records and they say that in the last 179 movies in which lawyers were portrayed, they were shown as dishonest 151 times. What should I say to them?"

Vetluguin sat there thinking a minute; then he turned to his assistant and said, "Tell them if those figures are right, the lawyers got a break."[4]

JUSTICE FOR ALL, EXCEPT . . .

A dual refrain of the bar is that lawyers are always ready to defend a client, no matter how unpopular—and that they deserve admiration for this principled stand. This, of course, is nonsense; the great majority of established lawyers will not go near any but the most respectable clients and cases. Even the country's biggest bar association does not live up to its own bombast. In 1950, the American Bar Association's House of Delegates, the group's parliament, decided to expel from the ABA any lawyer "who is a member of the Communist Party of the United States or who advocates Marxism-Leninism."

Three years later, the ABA carried its inquisition even further and urged the profession to disbar Communist lawyers.[5]

LEGAL SERVICES

The idea of providing legal services for the poor goes back over a hundred years, but until recently those services were all but nonexistent. In 1919, $181,408 was spent, and less than 200 lawyers worked, nationwide, on legal aid to the poor.[6]

Raynor Gardiner, general counsel of the Boston Legal Aid Society in1952, said:

> . . . *The great majority of our citizens have no access to legal aid and to pretend anything else is just pompous nonsense.*[7]

During the 1950s, the Bar Association fought tooth and nail against federal funding for free or subsidized legal services. The ABA passed a resolution stating that such government funding posed a "threat to individual freedom." A former president of the Association went so far as to say that "the greatest threat aside from the undermining influence of Communist infiltration is the propaganda campaign for a federal subsidy to finance a nationwide plan for legal aid and low-cost legal services." [8]

In 1960, there was one legal aid lawyer for every 120,000 people living in poverty—while there was one lawyer for 560 people in the general population. As late as 1964, only $4 million was being spent on legal aid—almost all from private funds.[9]

TRICKS OF A SORDID TRADE

Martin Mayer, in his exposé *The Lawyers*, published in 1967, reveals some of the secret codes and signs used by the legal cabal in the1950s and '60s:

An older New York lawyer with little experience in the criminal courts had a client who had been picked up in another county for drunk driving, and for whom a conviction at precisely this moment would be extremely inconvenient. He wanted a postponement, but knew of no excuse a judge would have to accept, so he consulted with the young assistant district attorney who would be on duty that day. The DA heard the reason for the postponement . . . and said, "That's all right. You just tell the judge you haven't been able to get hold of your witness, Mr. Green."

"But I don't have any witness Mr. Green."

The DA looked incredulously at the older lawyer's white hairs and said, "Don't you know? It means you haven't been paid. Any judge will give an adjournment on that."

In Washington, DC, these matters are handled with greater formality: a lawyer still waiting for a fee comes into court and demands an adjournment "pursuant to Rule I of this Court."[10] According to an understandably anonymous Superior Court Judge, Rule I is still invoked in our nation's capital today.

THE BRASS CHECK

Not surprisingly, the 1960s generated a great deal of criticism of lawyers and the legal system they worked in and supported. One of the most striking rebukes of the era came from radical lawyer Florynce Kennedy, in an article entitled "The Whorehouse Theory of Law:"

The system of justice, and most especially the legal profession, is a whorehouse serving those best able to afford the luxuries of justice offered to preferred customers. The lawyer, in these terms, is analogous to a prostitute. The difference between the two is simple. The prostitute is honest—the buck is her aim. The lawyer is dishonest—he claims that justice, service to mankind, is his primary purpose.[11]

JUDGING JUDGES

Yippie and Grumpy

In 1968, just before the Chicago Conspiracy trial of the eight famous defendants charged with inciting a riot at the Democratic National Convention began, Judge Julius Hoffman was summoned from his home to hear an emergency defense motion on a Saturday afternoon. The motion was entered, not by one of the regular defense attorneys but by a young man in blue jeans with a long reddish beard.

He was a recent law school graduate, not yet licensed to practice in Illinois but awaiting the results of his Washington, DC bar exam. The young man explained that he was there merely to file the motion on behalf of William Kunstler, who was out of town.

"I will hear what you have to say," Judge Hoffman said, "not as a lawyer, but as a human being."13

"All in all I'd rather have been a judge than a miner. And what is more, being a miner, as soon as you are too old and tired and sick and stupid to do the job properly, you have to go. Well, the very opposite applies with judges."

Peter Cook,
'60s nightclub
entertainer12

LAWYERS ABOVE THE LAW

Setting minimum fees for all common legal services such as divorces, wills, bankruptcy and probate was standard practice among lawyers until recently—and the American Bar Association even formalized this racket in its Canon of Ethics, despite an obvious conflict with antitrust laws. In fact, the ABA declared it a breach of professional conduct not to adhere to minimum fees. Public criticism of this practice grew in the 1950s and '60s. Philip Stern, in his book *Lawyers on Trial*, describes how the bar rationalized this violation of the law:

> *The rule was nothing if not audacious. If any other industry had done what the lawyers did—that is, published minimum rates and threatened to discipline those who violated them—they would clearly have been violating the antitrust laws . . . but that did not seem to faze the legal profession. Bar leaders asserted that lawyers, being a learned profession and not engaged in mere commerce, were beyond the reach of antitrust laws.14*

In 1971, Lewis Goldfarb of Fairfax, Virginia, brought an antitrust suit against the lawyer's practice of setting minimum fees. Four years later, the U.S. Supreme Court banned minimum fee schedules, calling them a "classic example of price-fixing."

TELLING IT LIKE IT IS

By the late '60s, the gleam of the lawyers' Golden Age grew dim indeed as diverse groups of old, poor and black people roiled up against the establishment founded and perpetuated by the legal community. Slowly, the growing discontented ranks were joined by unlikely bedfellows: businesspeople, politicians and even lawyers themselves.

In April, 1969, thirteen members of the New York Chapter of the Black Panther party were arrested and subsequently charged with 156 felony counts. The trial lasted over a year and ended with the jury acquitting the Panthers on all counts. Afterward, a number of jurors openly expressed their opinion that the judge, Supreme Court Judge John Murtagh, had shown bias during the trial. During pre-trial hearings the defendants sent a letter to Murtagh, condemning not only the judge, but the entire American legal system as racist:

In the North, in the South, in the East and in the West, all over the country, Black people are accused of crimes, thrown into your jails, dragged through your courts and administered a sour dose of "American justice." We are in jail outside, and in jail inside. Black people and now all poor people have been well educated in the American school of justice . . . .

Accusations of contempt for the "dignity" of and lack of respect for the court indicate to us, the defendants, that a devious attempt by the court prevails to obscure the truth of these proceedings. There is a glaring distinction between theory and practice within the "halls of justice" which is consistent with judicial history as it pertains to Black and poor people . . . What fool cannot see that the "justice" of which you speak has a dual interpretation quite apart from the legal definition and is in keeping with "slave-master" traditions? . . .

This court represents the most ruthless system in the world, caring nothing for the wholesale misery that it brings, while at the same time your papers are full of verbiage of your "nobility," "righteousness," "justice," "fairness" and the "good" that you do.[15]

> *"By and large . . . big-city criminal administration is a jungle, a snake pit, an aggregation of horrors. It is a dismal swamp of no-hope for the offenders who make the process necessary. It is a livable turf for mean, venal and small-time chiselers whose only qualification is a license to practice law."*
>
> Abe Fortas
> (1910-1982),
> Associate Justice of the
> U.S. Supreme Court [16]

HONEST TO HIS FAULT

F. Lee Bailey (1933 -   ), is one of America's most notorious trial lawyers. And he's successful enough to be honest about his trade:

*Those who think the information brought out at a
criminal trial is the truth, the whole truth and nothing
but the truth, are fools. Prosecuting or defending a case
is nothing more than getting to those people who will
talk for your side, who will say what you want said.*[17]

and

*The public regards lawyers with great distrust. They
think lawyers are smarter than the average guy, but use
their intelligence deviously. Well, they're wrong: Usually
they're not smarter.*[18]

JUSTICE FOR SALE

Jerry Rubin, once a Yippie agitator, remarked in 1970 on
the plea-bargaining system in American courts:

*Justice in America is a supermarket . . . The judge is a
poker player and the cards are other people's lives. It's
blackmail. If we demand our constitutional rights—a
jury trial—we pay even more heavily when found guilty.*

*The courtroom is a negotiating session between the State
and criminal on how much the criminal must pay for
having been arrested. Ninety-five percent of the people
busted make deals to get lesser punishments. The poor
stand helpless in the face of the state's power. The rich
get rich man's justice; the poor get poor man's justice.*[19]

THE SCANDAL SHEET

Watergate

With only a couple of exceptions, every major figure
involved in the scandal that began with the 1972 break-in of the
Watergate Hotel was a lawyer. This besmirched group of attor-
neys, enough to stock a reasonably-sized firm, included G.
Gordon Liddy, John Dean, Charles Colson, Spiro Agnew, Egil
Krogh, Jr., Attorney-General John Mitchell, John Ehrlichman,
Herbert Kalmbach, Robert Mardian, Edwin Reinecke, Donald
Segretti and, of course, Duke University Law School, Class of
'37, Richard Nixon.[20]

WOULD-BE PRESIDENTIAL WISDOM

Politics as it is practiced in the United States . . . is a beautiful fraud that has been imposed on the people for years, whose practitioners exchange gilded promises for the most valuable thing their victims own, their votes. And who benefits most? The lawyers.

Shirley Chisholm, U.S. Representative and presidential candidate (1924-) [21]

ROGUES GALLERY

Roy Marcus Cohn (1927-1986)

> *"Do not waste your time looking up the law in advance, because you can find some federal district court that will sustain any proposition you make."*
>
> Senator Sam Ervin
> (1896- 1985)[22]

Roy Cohn shot to national fame in 1953 as chief counsel to Senator Joe McCarthy's anti-communist inquisition, becoming notorious as an arrogant and brilliant lawyer—a reputation he milked for a lifetime, although he was at bottom a lazy, unprincipled crook.

Cohn's character was evident from an early age. As a teenager, he used his father's notoriety as a judge to squash his teachers' traffic tickets. He rode to high school in a limousine.

He graduated from Columbia Law School at twenty, and had to wait a year before he could be admitted to practice law. Political connections soon got him a job in New York as an Assistant United States Attorney, where he had the opportunity to work on several prominent cases, including the trial of Julius and Ethel Rosenberg. In 1950, he was transferred to Washington, and by 1953 had become Sancho Panza to McCarthy's wild Quixote. But when the Army-McCarthy hearings brought down his boss, Cohn was driven out of Washington and out of a job.

He returned to New York, the most forgiving of cities, and soon landed a job at Saxe, Bacon & Bolan, where he remained until his disbarment thirty years later. The firm was home base for Cohn's hobnobbing, power-broking, string-pulling and—incidentally it seemed—law practice. It was also, particularly in Cohn's later years, something of a front. Clients who thought they were paying top dollar for mogul Cohn were actually receiving the services of neophytes. The *American Lawyer* magazine revealed that:

> *. . . while Cohn was out rainmaking [drumming up business], a cadre of law students and first-, second-, and third-year associates would be handling most of the*

work . . . . It was, according to Cohn's youthful subordinates, lawyering on the cheap, and it caused a constant turnover as young attorneys burned out after a few years of heavy caseloads, poor clerical backup, long hours, and low pay.[23]

A co-worker recalled: "When Roy was at Le Cirque we'd all be at our desks eating cheeseburgers."[24]

That may have been just as well. Though he cultivated a reputation as a tough, brilliant courtroom performer, there was little substance behind the swagger. Actually, he hated doing pretrial research, was rarely prepared in court, and was often an ineffective and unorganized strategist. "Roy would have been a great lawyer," said one colleague, "if he'd ever cracked a law book."[25] And gossip columnist Liz Smith, a friend of longstanding, averred: "He was a wonderful intimidator and bluffer and bullshit artist. I don't think . . . that he could write a paper or draft anything."[26]

Cohn preferred using subterfuges and lawyerly tricks before a trial, indulging in postponements, delays and technicalities to wear out the other side and force a settlement. Said one lawyer who worked with him:

The strategy was to squeeze: once we got the injunction, adjournments, delays, motions brought in front of other judges to screw things up so another judge would be called in . . . . Once he had those initial handcuffs on the other side, he would delay, delay, and delay . . . .

Cohn was inordinately proud of what he thought was his tremendous ability to speak in court without notes or preparation. But, continued the same lawyer:

As far as working with him, he would take a memo that I or someone else had put together on a case, he would scan it, and then he would just proceed to ad-lib and he would take it from there. A lot of people were somehow impressed by his presence, but anyone who had their brains would know he was full of bullshit.[27]

Cohn's practice included a penchant for bribing judges, submitting false affidavits and using political pull inside the courtroom. A typical example of his malpractice was in the case he handled for Adele Holzer, a Broadway producer indicted for grand larceny in connection with money raised for a theatrical production. Holzer paid Cohn a fee of $24,000. The lawyer did no preparation at all. As the trial date approached, Cohn told the judge the case had become a burden and asked to be relieved of it—a request the judge refused to grant.

Holzer eventually got to see one of Cohn's young subordinates for one hour before the start of the trial, an interview that constituted the defense's entire preparation. Cohn showed up for part of the trial—but only after Holzer had paid him an additional $4,000. For that he examined her and three other witnesses and delivered half of the defense's summation. Holzer was convicted, but she wasn't through with Cohn's incompetence yet. Because he forgot to file a routine notice of appeal, Holzer unexpectedly was shipped off to Riker's Island prison that very afternoon. "A prudent attorney," explained one New York lawyer, "would come to the sentencing with the notice of appeal and a motion for a stay of execution in hand. A prudent attorney would also request that the prosecutor go with him to the appeals court judge to ensure that things went smoothly."[28] But no one ever accused Roy Cohn of being a prudent attorney.

In addition to his law practice, Cohn ran a number of other money-making con games. He was involved in a tangle of corporations, partnerships and schemes— some legal, some not— including several check-cashing and food stamp outlets, two pornographic theaters, parking lots and more. These extralegal and illegal activities, in fact, were much more lucrative than his law practice.

Cohn had another novel way of increasing his net worth: He didn't pay his bills. Throughout his career, he was known as a tremendous, indeed superlative, deadbeat. In a 1979 investigation, the *New York Daily News* turned up forty-seven court judgments filed against him—and there were likely many more creditors who had just written off the money.

It was this bad habit that became the main impetus for Cohn's disbarment. In 1966, he had borrowed $100,000 from a client, Iva Schlesinger. Nearly twenty years later, the loan was still unpaid, and Schlesinger filed a complaint with the Bar Association's Disciplinary Committee. Uncharacteristically, the committee swung into action. Cohn had filed an affidavit in which he said the money was not a loan, but a payment for legal services. Unfortunately for him, Schlesinger had saved twenty years' of correspondence regarding the transaction, in which Cohn had repeatedly referred to the money as a loan. The rogue was finally caught red-handed. There were a couple of other charges as well, one that he had lied on a bar application, another that he had coerced a dying and mentally incapicitated friend, Lewis Rosenstiel, into signing a will that made Cohn a trustee of Rosenstiel's estate. On June 23, 1986, Cohn was disbarred.

A lifetime ultra-conservative, Cohn was an active campaigner against gay rights. He lobbied against the New York

"Lawyer: An individual whose principal role is to protect his clients from others of his profession."

Anonymous

City gay rights ordinance, gave speeches about the threat of homosexual teachers in the schools and spoke contemptuously of "fags." But in fact, and in keeping with his unremitting hypocrisy, Cohn was gay himself. He died of AIDS on August 2, 1986.

LENGTHY BRIEFS

As the number of lawyers grows arithmetically, the amount of printed material generated by them seems to increase geometrically. Arthur Vanderbilt, the Chief Justice of New Jersey, listed:

> . . . *The judicial decisions, constitutions and statutes, administrative rules and rulings, and the mass of secondary authorities such as digests, encyclopedias, annotated cases, volumes of citations, treatises, restatements and law reviews . . . The first thing about our legal system that strikes a European or Latin-American lawyer is its sheer bulk.*[29]

And even a North American would be struck by the bulkiness achieved by Arnold S. Jacobs, an adjunct professor at New York Law School. He recently wrote a 500-page article for the school's law review on Section 16 of the Securities and Exchange Act. This exegesis contains a mind-boggling 4,824 footnotes.[30]

BUSINESS AS USUAL

Under the Legal Services Program, which was established in 1964, the number of cases litigated for the poor tripled. Whereas previously, no legal aid case had ever been before the U.S. Supreme Court, in the ten years of its existence, the Legal Services Program brought 164 such cases, winning 74. Many people in government and business—the objects of many of these suits—felt that the program was becoming far too enthusiastic in its defense of the legal rights of the poor.

In 1974, the Legal Services Program was eliminated and the Legal Services Corporation formed. The Corporation had a much narrower focus than the Program. Although more expensive, the Corporation has been much less effective in defending the rights of poor people.

The total amount of money spent on legal aid was still very small. For example, in 1977, American corporations spent $24 billion on legal services. At the same time, the Legal Services Corporation was spending about $300 million—approximately $10 for each of the thirty million Americans living in poverty.

"Some men are heterosexual, and some are bisexual, and some men don't think about sex at all . . . they become lawyers."

Woody Allen (1935-), comedian and director[31]

Under the Reagan administration, spending for legal aid was cut by $100 million, The theory was that public-spirited lawyers would rush to pick up the slack by offering free legal services to the poor.[32]

We're still waiting.

PRESIDENTIAL WISDOM

"Ninety percent of our lawyers serve ten percent of our people. We are over-lawyered and under-represented."
Jimmy Carter (1924-), Thirty-ninth President, in a speech before the Los Angeles County Bar Association on May 4, 1978 [34]

THE SELFLESS LAWYER

Art Buchwald (1925-), columnist and social critic, made the following comments in a commencement address to the Tulane University School of Law, Class of '79:

It is an honorable calling that you have chosen. Some of you will soon be defending poor, helpless insurance companies who are constantly being sued by greedy, vicious widows and orphans trying to collect on their policies. Others will work tirelessly to protect frightened, beleaguered oil companies from being attacked by depraved consumer groups. A few of you will devote your lives to suing doctors, while many of you will choose to sue the patients.[35]

WITH PROBLEMS LIKE THIS, WHO NEEDS SOLUTIONS?

The *National Law Journal* recently asked chief justices in all U.S. jurisdictions about their major concerns. Were it only that more could echo the complaints of the Chief Justices of American Samoa:

Our caseload is pitiful. Our main problem is getting reluctant litigants into court. Samoans are great at compromising. It is part of their culture to talk things out. As a result, most cases are settled out of court with no intervention by the judge.[36]

DISCIPLINARY INACTION

Imagine that you hire a plumber to do some work in your house. The plumber then sends you a bill for work that was not done, or done so shoddily that you have to have it redone, or uses the access to your house to steal from you. You decide to file a complaint with the appropriate state agency to have the plumber's license revoked.

You find, to your surprise, that you must file your complaint not with the state, but with a committee set up by the plumbers' union. All the individuals investigating your charges are plumbers, those who make the ruling are plumbers, and when they have made a determination, it is then rubber-stamped by a state agency, also made up of plumbers. Unfortunately for plumbers, it is not that easy; their occupation is regulated by state licensing and contractors' agencies.

But fortunately for those in the legal profession, as implausible as it seems, errant lawyers are disciplined by other lawyers. As Philip Stern put it:

> . . . the power to write the rules lawyers must follow . . .
> is vested, for all practical purposes, not in publicly
> elected or appointed city or state officials, but in the
> lawyers' private trade organizations: the bar
> associations, national, state and local.[37]

In 1970, the ABA set up a committee to study its own disciplinary enforcement. The investigation was headed by former Supreme Court Justice Tom C. Clark. The group reported:

> With few exceptions, the prevailing attitude of lawyers
> toward disciplinary enforcement ranges from apathy to
> outright hostility. Disciplinary action is practically non-
> existent in many jurisdictions.[38]

The Clark Report also noted that lawyers disbarred in one community continued to practice by moving to another, that lawyers convicted of serious crimes, including grand larceny of clients' funds, were allowed to continue practicing while they appealed—a process which often took three or four years.

The report had almost no impact on disciplinary proceedings. Eight years later, the ABA reported—in fact bragged, in a press release—that of the 450,000 lawyers practicing in the United States at that time, only 503 had received public disciplinary action of any kind, and only 124 had been disbarred.[39] These low figures are not due to a lack of complaints about legal services. In 1984, the California bar alone received 8,329

"Poor people have access to American courts in the same sense that the Christians had access to the lions when they were dragged into a Roman arena."

Judge Earl Johnson, Jr. (1933-)[33]

complaints from clients against lawyers, but dismissed 97 percent of them.

Of course, the reason so many complaints are dismissed, and so little action is taken, and so few disbarments take place, could possibly be that innocent lawyers are constantly being falsely accused by conniving and duplicitous clients.

But a more plausible explanation is given by Laurens Schwartz (1951-), in his recent work *What You Aren't Supposed to Know About the Legal Profession:*

> *". . . the code of ethics (or professional responsibility) is not geared toward the behavior of lawyers themselves. The code is a public relations device aimed at making lawyers look decorous and above-board to the general public, consisting of potential clients . . ."*[40]

Or, as Sydney J. Harris bluntly put it:

> *Bar associations are notoriously reluctant to disbar or even suspend a member unless he has murdered a judge downtown at high noon, in the presence of the entire committee on Ethical Practices.*[41]

THE NUMBER YOU HAVE DIALED IS NOT IN SERVICE. . .

In 1986, the California State Bar set up a toll-free number for people to call to make complaints about lawyers, but they didn't publicize it—it was not even available from Directory Assistance—because to do so would have increased the number of complaints too much.[42]

WHEN THE BAR GETS TOUGH, THE TOUGH DON'T GET DISBARRED

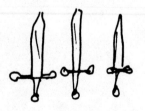

Responding to criticism that the bar's disciplinary procedures were too lenient, the California State Bar recently revamped its system to make it tougher on errant attorneys. In one of the first findings under the new rules, a state bar review panel recommended against disbarment for a lawyer convicted of hiring a gunman to kill a client, citing "mitigating circumstances." [43]

Perhaps, like the British Admiralty, the bar approves of killing a client now and again to encourage the others.

THE ONE GREAT PRINCIPLE OF LAW: GET THE FEE FIRST

It is well known that lawyers charge by the hour. What is less appreciated is that the lawyer's hour is not the same as the hour of the normal human being. The lay hour has 60 minutes, no more, no less. That of the lawyer is more flexible. Recently, for example, a West Virginia lawyer billed his client for a 74-hour day, claiming 22 hours of travel and 52 hours of court time. In another well-known case, the Pennzoil-Texaco litigation, one apparently tireless attorney billed Texaco for 24 hours of work on two consecutive days.[44]

Some of the ways that lawyers play both fast and loose with billing practices are:

Unit Billing

When a client calls a lawyer on the phone or drops into the office, he or she will probably be billed at fifteen or thirty-minute intervals. For example, if a client calls with a question about a case, and the call takes three minutes, that call will be billed at fifteen minutes of "lawyer time." If the lawyer fields five such calls in a fifteen minute period, the "legal" hour is already seventy-five minutes long and only one-quarter gone.[45]

Billing Lawyer Rates for Routine Office Work

A large number of firms bill for the hourly rate of a lawyer, no matter who actually does the work. Routine legal work is almost always done by a legal secretary or paralegal whose labor, needless to say, does not cost the firm anywhere near the billed rate.[46]

Efficiency Billing

Like all professionals, lawyers tend to specialize in particular tasks—for example, filing patent applications or estate planning. Of course, after a certain amount of time, they get more efficient at handling such cases. Some lawyers, though, will charge for the number of hours it takes an inexperienced or fair-to-middling lawyer to do the work. Their rationale is that they should not suffer for being good at their job. This would be funny, if it weren't true.[47]

Double Billing

When lawyers have to travel a long distance to handle a case, they often arrange to take care of two or three cases on the same trip. This makes perfect sense. What doesn't make perfect sense is to bill each client for the entire trip. Yet this is exactly what many do.[48]

Charges for Expenses

You might think that someone making $250 an hour might not mind picking up the cost of paperclips. You think wrong. In addition to hourly fees, many law firms charge their clients for everything from photocopies to after-hours office air-conditioning. Lawyers realized that their clients don't pay much attention to a charge if it is listed as an expense.

Some firms figure out what the extra services cost them, and just pass the expense on to clients. Others include a markup. In Los Angeles, for example, it is not uncommon for a firm to charge 25 cents a page for photocopying. These "extras" can account for as much as ten percent of a firm's total revenue.[49]

THE NET RESULT IS BORING

Derek C. Bok, the President of Harvard Law School, made the following remarks in 1981:

> Not only does the law absorb many more young people
> in America than in any other industrialized nation, it
> attracts an unusually large proportion of the
> exceptionally gifted . . . . The share of all Rhodes
> scholars who go on to law school has approximated 40
> percent in recent years, dwarfing the figures for any
> other occupational group . . . .
>
> The net result . . . is a massive diversion of exceptional
> talent into pursuits that often add little to the growth of
> the economy, the pursuit of culture, or the enhancement
> of the human spirit. [50]

"I decided law was the exact opposite of sex; even when it was good, it was lousy."

Mortimer Zuckerman, (1937-), ex-lawyer[51]

THE BATTLE OF BRITAIN REVISITED

In 1985, the American Bar Association held its annual meeting in London. A column by Miles Kington in *The Times* of London warned his readers about the most dangerous invasion since 1066:

> The American Bar Association is holding its annual
> shindig in London this year starting today. That means
> there are 20,000 American lawyers on the loose.
>
> These men are dangerous. If you should see one, do not
> have a go. Above all else, do not have a go. Lay a finger
> on any of them and they will sue for $11 million. Why
> $11 million? Nobody knows, but this is the sum that
> American lawyers sue people for, no matter what the
> supposed offence is.
>
> This trip has cost them a lot of money. Somehow, they
> have to get that money back. How will they do it? By

*suing you, of course, and it's no use your saying you
haven't done anything they could sue you for. These
guys know all the twists and turns. Take the following
scenario, for example:*

American*: Pardon me, sir, but could you direct my
wife and me to Buckingham Court?*

You*: (knowing full well that he means Buckingham
Palace): Why, certainly, my good fellow. Get on any bus
to Harrods, walk up the road and down through the
park and there you are.*

American*: You are very kind. May we exchange
addresses so that we can come and visit with you?*

*What he knows, and you don't is that there is a
Buckingham Court in London NW4 There will shortly
be arriving at your address a writ for culpable waste of
time, amounting to the exact amount of $11 million.*[52]

OH BILLY, YOU'RE BREAKIN' ME HEART!

In 1985, William Foltz, Chairman of the ABA's Delivery of
Legal Services Committee, said he was distressed that media do
not report about the many public-spirited things lawyers do,
including "the lack of recognition accorded to indigent defense
lawyers, often paid just $40 to $50 per hour."[53]

MAMA, DON'T LET YOUR BABIES GROW UP TO BE LAWYERS

According to a recent poll commissioned by the *National
Law Journal,* nine out of ten parents interviewed would not
want their child to grow up to be a lawyer.[54]

In another survey, only 19 percent credited lawyers with
"high or very high" ethical standards, ranking them below
druggists, dentists and funeral directors. In yet another, only 12
percent expressed a "great deal of confidence" in lawyers—last
out of fifteen major institutions studied.[55]

WHAT GOES AROUND COMES AROUND

Art Buchwald points out the disadvantages of malpractice
suits in this piece: "The Case of the Lawyer's Kidneys:"

It had to happen soon or later. Lawyer Dobbins was wheeled into the emergency room on a stretcher, rolling his head in agony. Doctor Green came over to see him.

"Dobbins," he said. "What an honor. The last time I saw you was in court when you accused me of malpractice."

"Doc, Doc. My side is on fire. The pain is right here. What could it be?"

"How would I know? You told the jury I wasn't fit to be a doctor."

"I was only kidding, Doc. When you represent a client you don't know what you're saying. Could I be passing a kidney stone?"

"Your diagnosis is as good as mine."

"What are you talking about?"

"When you questioned me on the stand you indicated you knew everything there was to know about the practice of medicine."

"Doc, I'm climbing the wall. Give me something."

"Let's say I give you something for a kidney stone and it turns out to be a gallstone. Who is going to pay for my court costs?"

"I'll sign a paper that I won't sue."

"Can I read to you from the transcript of the trial? Lawyer Dobbins: 'Why were you so sure my client had tennis elbow?' Dr. Green: 'I've treated hundreds of people with tennis elbow, and I know it when I see it.' Dobbins: 'It never occured to you my client could have Excedrin headache?' Green: 'No, sir . . . There were no signs of an Excedrin headache.' Dobbins: 'You and your ilk make me sick.'"

"Why are you reading that to me?"

"Because, Dobbins, since the trial I've lost confidence in making a diagnosis. A lady came in the other day limping . . . ."

"Please, Doc, I don't want to hear it now. Give me some Demerol."

"You said during the suit that I dispensed drugs like a drunken sailor. I've changed my ways, Dobbins. I don't prescribe drugs anymore."

"Then get me another doctor."

"There are no other doctors on duty. The reason I'm here is that after the malpractice suit the sheriff seized everything in my office. This is the only place I can practice." [56]

BUT M*A*S*H WAS ON THAT NIGHT

Out of the 20,000 lawyers who attended the American Bar Association convention in San Francisco in 1987, a panel on how to provide better legal access to the public drew a crowd of twelve.[57]

SEN. ESQ.

Lawyers are found, in inordinate numbers, at all levels of government, from city school board to Chief Executive. Senator Eugene McCarthy (1916-), in his autobiography *Up Til Now: A Memoir*, describes that most fearsome of creations, the Lawyer-Senator—outmonstered only by the Lawyer-President:

Another group in the Senate were the self-conscious lawyers, distinguished by their disposition in debate or argument to preface their remarks with "speaking as a lawyer" or "thinking as a lawyer" as though this condition adds special weight to what they might have to say.

Occasionally, I would question one of these lawyer speakers as to how I, a nonlawyer, should interpret his remarks. Was I to assume that I could not understand what he was about to say, or what he had said, because of my nonlawyer status? Or would he explain, if he could, in nonlegal terms, or nonlawyer terms, what he had said, so that I might better understand his remarks? Or, I might ask how he thought differently as a lawyer than he did when he shifted into his nonlawyer mind, and would he tell me when he had made the shift so that I could tune in properly?

"Just when I thought there was no way to stop the Japanese from steadily widening their lead over American industry, I saw a headline in the paper that said 'JAPAN TO OPEN ITS DOOR TO AMERICAN LAWYERS.' That ought to do it."[57]

Calvin Trillin (1935-)

None of the lawyer members who used this device ever gave me a satisfactory explanation, although while trying one or the other might slip in a few Latin terms like ad hoc *or* duces tecum *as special marks of distinction.*[58]

LEGAL LYRICS

Frances Norris has translated Joyce Kilmer's famous poem "Trees" into Legalese in a piece entitled "Legal Trees:"

(In homage to Joyce Kilmer; pursuant to Section 103 of Copyright Laws—Title 17, U.S. Code—heretofore referenced under the pains and penalties of plagiarism.)

I think that I shall never see,
Notwithstanding any past, present, or future visions,
A poem lovely as a tree—the word tree
Used herein to include her, his or its respective
Limbs, leaves, bark, roots,
Sap (if said tree proves maple), knotholes,
Birds, squirrels, insects, agents and servants.
If more than one tree is mentioned herein,
The images, similes, metaphors, and allusions
Shall be the joint and several obligations of each such tree
Through no fault of its own.
A tree whose hungry mouth is prest [sic]
Against the earth's sweet flowing breast
In the event that no receptacles, vehicles, baby carriages,
Or other like equipment
Obstruct the common ground as heretofore described.
A tree that, pursuant to religious beliefs
not set forth herein, looks at God all day,
And lifts her, his or its leafy arms, in a manner authorized
Under lawful covenant, to pray.
A tree that may in Summer wear,
To the most practical extent under the circumstances,
A nest of robins in her, his or its hair;
Provided that the aforementioned birds,
Their spouses, friends, relatives, invitees, visitors,
Agents, servants, and any offspring born to them
Shall neither make nor suffer any noisy, unclean,
Or otherwise offensive use of said tree.
Upon whose bosom snow has lain;
Who intimately lives with rain, hereupon and until
The reasonable cessation of said rain,
Or until the expiration and termination of said tree
By exercise of the power of eminent terrain,
Or by the action and authority of strong wind, lightning,

Chain saw, Dutch elm disease (if said tree proves Dutch
elm),
Or any other natural or unnatural force,
Unless otherwise stipulated in writing.
Poems are made by fools like me,*
But only God,
And no other instrument of like tenor,
Can make a legal tree.
*Subject to applicable law[59]

TELLTALE SIGNS

In the spring of 1988, a man was arrested in New York for impersonating a lawyer over a lengthy period. Assistant Manhattan District Attorney Brian Rosner said one judge told him:

"I should have suspected he wasn't a lawyer. He was always so punctual and polite."[60]

THIS IS A DAY UNTO THE LAWYER

In most of the world, the first day of May is Labor Day, honoring the International Worker. In the United States, since 1958, this day has been Law Day. David Margolick, in an article in *The New York Times*, discusses this popular holiday:

Law Day was the 1957 brainchild of a Washington, DC lawyer, Charles S. Rhyne, president of the ABA. It wasn't an easy sell. Sherman Adams told Mr. Rhyne that President Eisenhower wouldn't sign anything glorifying lawyers . . . . But the President concurred, and May 1, 1958 was the first Law Day.

The bar association spends $100,000 a year promoting Law Day, offering videotapes, brochures and other literature...There are also Law Day trinkets: Law Day bumper stickers, balloons and buttons ($6.00 per package); Law Day pencils ($6.00 for 50, unsharpened); Law Day plastic mugs ($1.00 each), Law Day greeting cards ($15.00 for a box of 25), and even Law Day litter bags ($6 for 50).

Mr. Rhyne was not invited to a White House ceremony last week where President Reagan signed a Law Day proclamation, but he says his idea has "turned out pretty well." William P. Rogers, who was Attorney-General in 1958, speculated his old boss would be "somewhat disappointed" that Law Day is barely noted.

*Asked how he planned to mark the occasion, he
hesitated. "When is it?" he asked. "I've forgotten which
day it is."*[61]

THE EVER-WAXING BAR

Breeding Like Rabbits, Spreading Like Plague

In 1989, the United States held over 750,000 practicing
lawyers, about one for every 350 people. In New York, one out
of every 230 inhabitants is a lawyer; in Washington DC, one out
of every twenty-two.

Compare these figures with the more fortunate Europeans:
in Great Britain, the ratio is one lawyer for every 1,500 citizens;
in Italy, 1 in 1,500; and in France, 1 in 6,000. Japan comes out
on top yet again: It has managed to keep its lawyer population
down to a startling and admirable one for every 14,000
people.[62]

NOTES

1 Bertram Hannett, *Law, Lawyers and Laymen: Making Sense of the American Legal System*, Harcourt Brace Jovanovich, New York, 1984, pg. 4.

2 E. Emmett Kane, M.D., "Jawbones and Sawbones" in William Lloyd Prosser, *The Judicial Humorist*, Little, Brown and Co., pgs. 30, 35-6.

3 Willie Sutton, *Where the Money Was: The Memoirs of a Bank Robber*, Viking Press, New York, 1976, pg. 28

4 "Legal Follies," *Nolo News*, Fall, 1987, pg. 24.

5 Mark Green, "The ABA as Trade Association," in Ralph Nader and Mark Green (eds.), *Verdicts on Lawyers*, Thomas Y. Crowell Co., New York, 1976, p. 208.

6 Susan E. Lawrence, *The Poor in Court* (doctoral dissertation, Johns Hopkins, 1985), University Microfilms, Ann Arbor, 1985, pg. 11.

7 Martin Mayer, *The Lawyers*, Harper and Row, 1967, New York, pg. 285.

8 Mark Kessler, *Legal Services for the Poor*, Greenwood Press, New York, 1982, pgs. 5-6.

9 Lawrence, *The Poor in Court*, pg. 18.

10 Mayer, *The Lawyers*, pg. 162.

11 Florynce Kennedy, "The Whorehouse Theory of Justice," quoted in Robert Lefcourt, (ed.), *Law Against the People: Essays to Demystify Law, Order and the Courts*, Random House, New York, 1971, pg. 81.

12 Fred Metcalf (ed.), *Penguin Book of Humorous Quotations*, Penguin, New York, 1986, pgs. 145-46.

13 J. Anthony Lukas, *The Barnyard Epithet and Other Obscenities: Notes on the Chicago Conspiracy Trial*, Harper and Row, New York, 1970, pg. 45.

14 Philip M. Stern, *Lawyers on Trial*, Times Books, New York, 1980, pg. 55.

15 "The Panther 21 to Judge Murtagh" in Robert Lefcourt (ed.), *Law Against the People*, Random House, New York, 1971, pgs. 194-95.

16 *San Francisco Examiner and Chronicle*, Nov. 3, 1974, "This World," pg. 2, quoted in Alan F. Pater and Jason R. Pater, *What They Said in 1970*, Monitor Book Co., Beverly Hills, 1971, pg. 189.

17 Pater and Pater, *What They Said in 1970*, pg. 206.

18 Pater and Pater, *What They said in 1972*, pg. 209.

19   Jerry Rubin, *Do It!*, Simon and Schuster, New York, 1970, pgs. 159-60. quoted in William Kunstler "In Defense of the Movement," in Lefcourt, *Law Against the People*, pg. 272.

20   Nader and Green (eds.) *Verdicts on Lawyers*, Thomas Y. Crowell Co., New York, 1976, pg. 47.

21   Shirley Chisholm, *Unbought and Unbossed*, (1970), Part. 1, Ch. 4, quoted in Elaine Partnow, *The Quotable Woman: 1800-On*, Anchor Press, Garden City, NY, 1979, pg. 376.

22   Dallas *Times Herald*, June 20, 1973, Section A, pg. 8, quoted in Pater and Pater, *What They Said in 1973*, pg. 225.

23   *The American Lawyer*, quoted in Nicholas von Hoffman, *Citizen Cohn*, Doubleday Books, New York, 1988, pgs. 380-81.

24   von Hoffman, *Citizen Cohn*, pg. 380.

25   von Hoffman, *Citizen Cohn*, pg. 75.

26   Liz Smith, quoted in von Hoffman, *Citizen Cohn*, pg. 386.

27   von Hoffman, *Citizen Cohn*, pg. 428.

28   von Hoffman, *Citizen Cohn*, pg. 430.

29   Mayer, *The Lawyers*, pgs. 418-9; Vanderbilt, *Man and Measures in the Law*, pg. 6.

30   *New York Daily News*, Dec. 19, 1988, pg. 6.

31   From Woody Allen, *Love, Sex, Death and the Meaning of Life, McGraw-Hill, New York, 1981*.

32   Stern, *Lawyers on Trial*, pgs. 6-7; Kessler, *Legal Services for the Poor*, pgs. 8-9.

33   Quoted in Edwin Chen, "The Poor Still Go Begging for Legal Help," *Los Angeles Times*, February 19, 1984, Part I, p. 8, from Becker, *On Trial*, pg.17.

34   Pater and Pater, *What They Said in 1978*, Moniter, 1978, pg. 166.

35   *Nolo News*, Spring, 1986, pg. 24

36   "Samoan Paradise," *Americans for Legal Reform*, Vol. 4, No. 4, Summer, 1984, pg. 16.

37   Stern, *Lawyers on Trial*, pg. 52.

38   ABA Special Committee on the Evaluation of Disciplinary Enforcement, *Problems and Recommendations in Disciplinary Enforcement*, Chicago, 1970, pg. 1. Quoted in Stern, *Lawyers on Trial*, pg. 82.

39   Stern, *Lawyers on Trial*, pg. 84.

40   Laurens R. Schwartz, *What You Aren't Supposed to Know About the Legal Profession*, Shapolsky Publishers, New York, 1988, pg. 151.

41   Murray Teigh Bloom, *Trouble with Lawyers*, Simon and
     Schuster, New York, 1968, pg. 157.

42   "Lawyer Complaints," *Nolo News*, Fall, 1987, pg. 4.

43   Katherine Bishop, "Moral Turpitude Case vs. Lawyers'
     Public Image" *New York Times*, Feb. 24, 1989, pg. B5.

44   "Time Barrier Broken by Lawyer," *Nolo News*, Winter, 1987,
     pg. 24.

45   Ralph Warner and Toni Ihara, *29 Reasons Not to Go to Law
     School*, Nolo Press, Berkeley, 1987, pg. 141.

46   Warner and Ihara, *29 Reasons Not to Go to Law School*, pg.
     141.

47   Warner and Ihara, *29 Reasons Not to Go to Law School*, pg.
     141.

48   Ralph Warner and Carol Pladsen, "Legal Fees: Get What
     You Pay For," *Nolo News*, Spring, 1984, pg. 17.

49   "Legal Follies," *Nolo News*, Fall, 87, pg. 24.

50   Derek C. Bok, "A Flawed System" *Harvard Magazine*,
     May/June 1983, pg. 41.

51   Warner and Ihara, *29 Reasons Not to Go to Law School*,
     pg.37.

52   *The Times*, June 15, 1985 quoted in "And from the London
     Times," *Nolo News*, Fall, 1985, pg. 20.

53   "The Poor Image of Lawyers," *Nolo News*, Fall, 1985, pg. 20.

54   "Poll: Wanna be a lawyer?," *New York Daily News*, Aug. 12,
     1986.

55   Mitchell E. Daniels, "The People's Bar Exam," *Americans for
     Legal Reform*, Vol. 7, No. 1, Fall, 86, pg. 5.

56   Art Buchwald, "The Case of the Lawyer's Kidneys,"
     Reprinted with permission of the author, *Los Angeles Times
     Syndicate*.

57   "Gossip," Vol. 7, No.3, *Nolo News*, Fall, 87, pg. 3.

58   Sen. Eugene McCarthy, from *Up Til Now: A Memoir* c 1987,
     reprinted in *Americans for Legal Reform*, Vol. 8, No. 3,
     April/June, 1988, pg 32.

59   Frances Norris, "Legal Trees," *The Atlantic*, June, 1988, pg.
     34.

60   "The Phony Lawyer Who Fooled 4 Judges" *San Francisco
     Chronicle*, May, 1988.

61   David Margolick, "At the Bar," *New York Times*, April 29,
     1988, pg. B 5.

62   Bertram Harnett, *Law, Lawyers and Laymen: Making Sense
     of the American Legal System*, Harcourt Brace Jovanovich,
     New York, 1984, pg. 37.

SUMMATION

Throughout these pages, we have watched the law and the lawyer develop, and heard the cries and protests of generations of victims and critics. The Anglo-Saxon trial by ordeal no longer exists, but a trial remains, if nothing else, an ordeal. One who goes to law is no longer in danger of losing a life, but the loss of one's livelihood is a distinct possibility.

The complex and nearly unintelligible legal system that developed in England during the Middle Ages is of course a thing of the past. Yet, despite centuries of alleged reform, our modern legal system continues to be complex and nearly unintelligible. And just as in England seven centuries ago, there are dozens of different court systems operating simultaneously in the United States—each with its own procedures and jurisdictions, rules and regulations.

The abolition, at the end of the Nineteenth Century, of special pleading, the practice of using specific and precise legal forms to commence a trial, was certainly an important reform. But then we find this disconcerting report from self-help law advocate Jake Warner:

> *In most states, documents for routine actions such as simple probate or child support modification to adjust for inflation must be typed on a weird sort of numbered paper used no place else in the world, following a bizarre format. Much of the language required (which, incidentally, legal secretaries slavishly copy from legal form books or, if they are current, download from computerized form generators) has so little real meaning that it has scarcely changed since the death of (or, for that matter, the birth) of Queen Victoria.*[1]

Somehow, this does not sound much like an improvement over the Nineteenth Century system of special pleading.

The Jacksonian ideal of *Every Man His Own Lawyer*—the conviction that lawyering should be accessible to everyone—is now the all but forgotten dream of a more egalitarian age. Worse: Access to the law by the nonlawyer is actually illegal in most states. Unauthorized practice of the law (UPL) rules typically prohibit nonlawyers even from such routine tasks as filling out legal forms or advising others on filing or court procedures. These rules are enforced by individuals sitting on courts, by members of UPL committees of the state bar associations and by public prosecutors—most of whom are lawyers.

Legal characters born in the Nineteenth and early Twentieth Centuries, such as the corporate lawyer continue to multiply apace. The sight of hundreds of lawyers drudging for a corporate client is not at all uncommon. When the investment banking firm Drexel, Burnham, Lambert Inc. faced charges from the Securities and Exchange Commission, it marshalled 115 lawyers to prepare its case; the SEC could afford only fifteen.[2] In 1988, Baker & McKenzie marked a legal milestone by becoming the first law firm to employ over 1,000 lawyers.[3]

From its crude beginnings at the turn of this century, ambulance-chasing also has flowered into a sophisticated art, though still startling in its crudity. The practice reached a new low when a poison gas leak killed nearly 2,000 and injured over 200,000 people in Bhopal, India in 1984. American lawyers not only rushed to the city in feverish anticipation of an immense windfall, but then, back in the United States, fell to loud public squabbling over who would be exclusive representatives of the victims and thereby exclusive recipients of the fees. Chief Justice Warren Burger called it an "unseemly, indeed shocking, spectacle."[4]

Perhaps there is an inevitable and never-ending animosity, one might say a class struggle, between the lawyer and the laity. No matter the century, or the country, or the circumstances, loathing and laughter can be found directed at the attorney.

The struggle continues.

LYING AHEAD...

By 1995, it is estimated that there will be one million lawyers in the United States. This frightening statistic inspired folksinger and satirist Tom Paxton to pen the following lament:

Humankind has survived some disasters for sure,
Like locusts and flash-floods and flu,
There's never a moment when we've been secure,
From the ills that the flesh is heir to.

If it isn't a war, it's some gruesome disease,
If it isn't disease, then it's war,
But there's worse still to come and I'm asking you please
How the world's gonna take any more?

In ten years we're gonna have one million lawyers,
One million lawyers, one million lawyers,
In ten years we're gonna have one million lawyers,
How much can a poor nation stand?

The world shook with dread of Atilla the Hun,
As he conquered with fire and steel,

And Genghis and Kublai and all of the Khans,
Ground a groaning world under the heel.

Disaster, disaster, so what else is new?
We've suffered the worst and then some.
So I'm sorry to tell you my suffering friends,
Of the terrible scourge still to come.

In ten years we're gonna have one million lawyers,
One million lawyers, one million lawyers,
In ten years we're gonna have one million lawyers,
How much can a poor nation stand?

Oh, a suffering world cries for mercy,
As far as the eye can see.
Lawyers around every bend in the road,
Lawyers in every tree.
Lawyers in restaurants, lawyers in clubs,
Lawyers behind every door,
Behind windows and potted plants, shade trees and shrubs,
Lawyers on pogo sticks, lawyers in politics!

In ten years we're gonna have one million lawyers,
One million lawyers, one million lawyers,
In ten years we're gonna have one million lawyers,
How much can a poor nation stand?
How much can a poor nation stand?[5]

NOTES

1 Ralph Warner, "More Access, Not More Lawyers," *Nolo News,* Nolo Press, Berkeley, Winter, 1987, pg. 9.

2 Thomas Mara, "Defending Drexel" in *Spy* magazine, Feb., 1989, pg. 101.

3 *National Law Journal,* Dec. 26, 1988, pg.11.

4 Warren Burger quoted in *New York Times*, Aug. 12, 1986, pg. 20.

5 Tom Paxton, "One Million Lawyers and Other Disasters," (c) Tom Paxton, Accabonac Music, ASCAP 1985.

THE END

INDEX BY AUTHOR

SOFTWARE

willmaker

Nolo Press/Legisoft

Recent statistics say chances are better than 2 to 1 that you haven't written a will, even though you know you should. WillMaker makes the job easy, leading you step by step in a fill-in-the-blank format. Once you've gone through the program, you print out the will and sign it in front of witnesses. Because writing a will is only one step in the estate planning process, WillMaker comes with a 200-page manual providing an overview of probate avoidance and tax planning techniques. National 3rd Ed.

Apple, IBM PC 5 1/4 & 3 1/2, Macintosh	$59.95
Commodore	$39.95

california incorporator

Attorney Mancuso and Legisoft, Inc.

About half of the small California corporations formed today are done without the services of a lawyer. This easy-to-use software program lets you do the paperwork with minimum effort. Just answer the questions on the screen, and California Incorporator will print out the 35-40 pages of documents you need to make your California corporation legal.

California Edition (IBM)	$129.00

the california nonprofit corporation handbook—computer edition with disk

Attorney Anthony Mancuso

This is the standard work on how to form a nonprofit corporation in California. Included on the disk are the forms for the Articles, Bylaws and Minutes you will need, as well as regular and special director and member minute forms. Also included are line-by-line instructions explaining how to apply for and obtain federal tax exempt status—this critical step applies to incorporating in all 50 states.

California 1st Ed.

IBM PC 5 1/4 & 3 1/2	$69.00
Macintosh	$69.00

how to form your own texas corporation—computer edition with disk

Attorney Anthony Mancuso

how to form your own new york corporation—computer edition with disk

Attorney Anthony Mancuso

More and more business people are incorporating to qualify for tax benefits, limited liability status, the benefit of employee status and financial flexibility. These software packages contain all the instructions, tax information and forms you need to incorporate a small business. All organizational forms are on disk.

1st Ed.

IBM PC 5 1/4 & 3 1/2	$69.00
Macintosh	$69.00

for the record

By attorney Warner & Pladsen

A book/software package that helps to keep track of personal and financial records; create documents to give to family members in case of emergency; leave an accurate record for heirs, and allows easy access to all important records with the ability to print out any section.

National Edition

Macintosh, IBM PC 5 1/4 & 3 1/2	$49.95

ESTATE PLANNING & PROBATE

nolo's simple will book

Attorney Denis Clifford

We feel it's important to remind people that if they don't make arrangements before they die, the state will give their property to certain close family members. If you want a particular person to receive a particular object, you need a will. It's easy to write a legally valid will using this book.

National 1st Ed.	$14.95

plan your estate: wills, probate avoidance, trusts & taxes

Attorney Denis Clifford

A will is only one part of an estate plan. The first concern is avoiding probate so that your heirs won't receive a greatly diminished inheritance years later. This book shows you how to create a "living trust" and gives you the information you need to make sure whatever you have saved goes to your heirs, not to lawyers and the government.

National 1st Ed.	$17.95

the power of attorney book

Attorney Denis Clifford

The Power of Attorney Book concerns something you've heard about but probably would rather ignore: Who will take care of your affairs, make your financial and medical decisions, if you can't? With this book you can appoint someone you trust to carry out your wishes.

National 2nd Ed.	$17.95

how to probate an estate

Julia Nissley

When a close relative dies, amidst the grieving there are financial and legal details to be dealt with. The natural response is to rely on an attorney, but that response can be costly. With How to Probate an Estate, you can have the satisfaction of doing the work yourself and saving those fees.

California 3rd Ed.	$24.95

the california nonprofit corporation handbook

Attorney Anthony Mancuso

Used by arts groups, educators, social service agencies, medical programs, environmentalists and many others, this book explains all the legal formalities involved in forming and operating a nonprofit corporation. Included are all the forms for the Articles, Bylaws and Minutes you will need. Also included are complete instructions for obtaining federal 501(c)(3) exemptions and benefits. The tax information in this section applies wherever your corporation is formed.

California 5th Ed. $29.95

how to form your own corporation

Attorney Anthony Mancuso

More and more business people are incorporating to qualify for tax benefits, limited liability status, the benefit of employee status and the financial flexibility. These books contain the forms, instructions and tax information you need to incorporate a small business.

California 7th Ed.	$29.95
Texas 4th Ed.	$24.95
New York 2nd. Ed.	$24.95
Florida 1st Ed.	$19.95

1988 calcorp update package

Attorney Anthony Mancuso

This update package contains all the forms and instructions you need to modify your corporation's Articles of Incorporation so you can take advantage of new California laws. $25.00

california professional corporation handbook

Attorney Anthony Mancuso

Health care professionals, marriage, family and child counsellors, lawyers, accountants and members of certain other professions must fulfill special requirements when forming a corporation in California. This edition contains up-to-date tax information plus all the forms and instructions necessary to form a California professional corporation. An appendix explains the special rules that apply to each profession.

California 3rd Ed. $29.95

marketing without advertising

Michael Phillips & Salli Rasberry

Every small business person knows that the best marketing plan encourages customer loyalty and personal recommendation. Phillips and Rasberry outline practical steps for building and expanding a small business without spending a lot of money.

National 1st Ed. $14.00

the partnership book

Attorneys Clifford & Warner

Lots of people dream of going into business with a friend. The best way to keep that dream from turning into a nightmare is to have a solid partnership agreement. This book shows how to write an agreement that covers evaluation of partner assets, disputes, buy-outs and the death of a partner.

National 3rd Ed. $18.95

nolo's small business start-up

Mike McKeever

Should you start a business? Should you raise money to expand your already running business? If the answers are yes, this book will show you how to write an effective business plan and loan package.

National 3rd Ed. $17.95

the independent paralegal's handbook: how to provide legal services without going to jail

Attorney Ralph Warner

A large percentage of routine legal work in this country is performed by typists, secretaries, researchers and various other law office helpers generally labeled paralegals. For those who would like to take these services out of the law office and offer them at a reasonable fee in an independent business, attorney Ralph Warner provides both legal and business guidelines.

National 1st Ed. $12.95

getting started as an independent paralegal (two audio tapes)

Attorney Ralph Warner

This set of tapes is a carefully edited version of Nolo Press founder Ralph Warner's Saturday Morning Law School class. It is designed for people who wish to go into business helping consumers prepare their own paperwork in uncontested actions such as bankruptcy, divorce, small business incorporations, landlord-tenant actions, probate, etc. Also covered are how to set up, run, and market your business, as well as a detailed discussion of Unauthorized Practice of Law.

National 1st Ed. $24.95

JUST FOR FUN

29 reasons not to go to law school

Ralph Warner & Toni Ihara

Lawyers, law students, their spouses and consorts will love this little book with its zingy comments and Thurberesque cartoons, humorously zapping the life of the law.—Peninsula Times Tribune Filled with humor and piercing observations, this book can save you three years, $70,000 and your sanity.

3rd Ed. $9.95

murder on the air

Ralph Warner & Toni Ihara

Here is a sure winner for any friend who's spent more than a week in the city of Berkeley...a catchy little mystery situated in the environs and the cultural mores of the People's Republic.—The Bay Guardian

Flat out fun...—San Francisco Chronicle $5.95

poetic justice

Ed. by Jonathan & Andrew Roth

A unique compilation of humorous quotes about lawyers and the legal system, from Socrates to Woody Allen. $8.95

collect your court judgment

Scott, Elias & Goldoftas

After you win a judgment in small claims, municipal or superior court, you still have to collect your money. Here are step-by-step instructions on hwo to collect your judgment from the debtor's bank accounts, wages, business receipts, real estate or other assets.
California 1st Ed. $24.95

make your own contract

Attorney Stephen Elias

Here are clearly written legal form contracts to: buy and sell property, borrow and lend money, store and lend personal property, make deposits on goods for later purchase, release others from personal liability, or pay a contractor to do home repairs.
National 1st Ed. $12.95

social security, medicare & pensions: a sourcebook for older americans

Attorney Joseph L. Matthews & Dorothy Matthews Berman

Social security, medicare and medicaid programs follow a host of complicated rules. Those over 55, or those caring for someone over 55, will find this comprehensive guidebook invaluable for understanding and utilizing their rightful benefits. A special chapter deals with age discrimination in employment and what to do about it.
National 4th Ed. $15.95

everybody's guide to small claims court

Attorney Ralph Warner

So, the dry cleaner ruined your good flannel suit. Your roof leaks every time it rains, and the contractor who supposedly fixed it won't call you back. The bicycle shop hasn't paid for the tire pumps you sold it six months ago. This book will help you decide if you have a case, show you how to file and serve papers, tell you what to bring to court, and how to collect a judgment.
California 8th Ed. $14.95
National 3rd Ed. $14.95

billpayers' rights

Attorneys Warner & Elias

Lots of people find themselves overwhelmed by debt. The law, however, offers a number of legal protections for consumers and Billpayers' Rights shows people how to use them.
Areas covered include: how to handle bill collectors, deal with student loans, check your credit rating and decide if you should file for bankruptcy.
California 8th Ed. $14.95

for sale by owner

George Devine

In 1986 about 600,000 homes were sold in California at a median price of $130,000. Most sellers worked with a broker and paid the 6% commission. For the median home that meant $7,800. Obviously, that's money that could be saved if you sell your own house. This book provides the background information and legal technicalities you will need to do the job yourself and with confidence.
California 1st Ed. $24.95

homestead your house

Attorneys Warner, Sherman & Ihara

Under California homestead laws, up to $60,000 of the equity in your home may be safe from creditors. But to get the maximum legal protection you should file a Declaration of Homestead before a judgment lien is recorded against you. This book includes complete instructions and tear-out forms.
California 7th Ed. $8.95

the landlord's law book: vol. 1, rights & responsibilities

Attorneys Brown & Warner

Every landlord should know the basics of landlord-tenant law. In short, the era when a landlord could substitute common sense for a detailed knowledge of the law is gone forever. This volume covers: deposits, leases and rental agreements, inspections (tenants' privacy rights), habitability (rent withholding), ending a tenancy, liability, and rent control.
California 2nd Ed. $24.95

the landlord's law book: vol. 2, evictions

Attorney David Brown

Even the most scrupulous landlord may sometimes need to evict a tenant. In the past it has been necessary to hire a lawyer and pay a high fee. Using this book you can handle most evictions yourself safely and economically.
California 2nd Ed. $24.95

tenants' rights

Attorneys Moskowitz & Warner

Your "security building" doesn't have a working lock on the front door. Is your landlord liable? How can you get him to fix it? Under what circumstances can you withhold rent? When is an apartment not "habitable?" This book explains the best way to handle your relationship with your landlord and your legal rights when you find yourself in disagreement.
California 10th Ed. $15.95

the deeds book: how to transfer title to california real estate

Attorney Mary Randolph

If you own real estate, you'll almost surely need to sign a new deed at one time or another. The Deeds Book shows you how to choose the right kind of deed, how to complete the tear-out forms, and how to record them in the county recorder's public records.
California 1st Ed. $15.95

dog law

Attorney Mary Randolph

There are 50 million dogs in the United States—and, it seems, at least that many rules and regulations for their owners to abide by. *Dog Law* covers topics that everyone who owns a dog, or lives near one, needs to know about disputes, injury or nuisance.

National 1st Ed. $12.95

the criminal records book

Attorney Warren Siegel

We've all done something illegal. If you were one of those who got caught, your juvenile or criminal court record can complicate your life years later. The good news is that in many cases your record can either be completely expunged or lessened in severity.

The Criminal Records Book takes you step by step through the procedures to: seal criminal records, dismiss convictions, destroy marijuana records, reduce felony convictions.

California 2nd Ed. $14.95

draft, registration and the law

Attorney R. Charles Johnson

This clearly written guidebook explains the present draft law and how registration (required of all male citizens within thirty days of their eighteenth birthday) works. Every available option is presented along with a description of how a draft would work if there were a call tomorrow.

National 2nd Ed. $9.95

fight your ticket

Attorney David Brown

At a trade show in San Francisco recently, a traffic court judge (who must remain nameless) told our associate publisher that he keeps this book by his bench for easy reference.

If you think that ticket was unfair, here's the book showing you what to do to fight it.

California 3rd Ed. $16.95

how to become a united states citizen

Sally Abel Schreuder

This bilingual (English/Spanish) book presents the forms, applications and instructions for naturalization. This step-by-step guide will provide information and answers for legally admitted aliens who wish to become citizens.

National 3rd Ed. $12.95

how to change your name

Attorneys Loeb & Brown

Wish that you had gone back to your maiden name after the divorce? Tired of spelling over the phone V-e-n-k-a-t-a-r-a-m-a-n S-u-b-r-a-m-a-n-i-a-m?

This book explains how to change your name legally and provides all the necessary court forms with detailed instructions on how to fill them out.

California 4th Ed. $14.95

legal research: how to find and understand the law

Attorney Stephen Elias

Legal Research could also be called Volume-Two-for-all-Nolo-Press-Self-Help-Law-Books. A valuable tool for paralegals, law students and legal secretaries, this book provides access to legal information—he legal self-helper can find and research a case, read statutes, and make Freedom of Information Act requests.

National 2nd Ed. $14.95

family law dictionary

Attorneys Leonard and Elias

Written in plain English (as opposed to legalese), the Family Law Dictionary has been compiled to help the lay person doing research in the area of family law (i.e., marriage, divorce, adoption, etc.). Using cross referencs and examples as well as definitions, this book is unique as a reference tool.

National 1st Edition $13.95

patent, copyright & trademark: intellectual property law dictionary

Attorney Stephen Elias

This book uses simple language free of legal jargon to define and explain the intricacies of items associated with trade secrets, copyrights, trademarks and unfair competition, patents and patent procedures, and contracts and warranties.—IEEE Spectrum

If you're dealing with any multi-media product, a new business product or trade secret, you need this book.

National 1st Ed. $17.95

the people's law review: an access catalog to law without lawyers

Edited by Attorney Ralph Warner

Articles, interviews and a resource list introduce the entire range of do-it-yourself law from estate planning to tenants' rights. The People's Law Review also provides a wealth of background information on the history of law, some considerations on its future, and alternative ways of solving legal problems.

National 1st Ed. $8.95

the living together kit
Attorneys Ihara & Warner
Few unmarried couples understand the laws that may affect them. Here are useful tips on living together agreements, paternity agreements, estate planning, and buying real estate.
National 5th Ed. $17.95

how to do your own divorce
Attorney Charles E. Sherman
This is the book that launched Nolo Press and advanced the self-help law movement. During the past 17 years, over 400,000 copies have been sold, saving consumers at least $50 million in legal fees (assuming 100,000 have each saved $500—certainly a conservative estimate).
California 15th Ed. $14.95
Texas 2nd Ed. (Sherman & Simons) $12.95

california marriage & divorce law
Attorneys Warner, Ihara & Elias
For a generation, this practical handbook has been the best resource for the Californian who wants to understand marriage and divorce laws. Even if you hire a lawyer to help you with a divorce, it's essential that you learn your basic legal rights and responsibilities.
California 10th Ed. $15.95

practical divorce solutions
Attorney Charles Ed Sherman
Written by the author of *How to Do Your Own Divorce* (with over 500,000 copies in print), this book provides a valuable guide both to the emotional process involved in divorce as well as the legal and financial decisions that have to be made.
California 1st Ed. $12.95

the guardianship book
Lisa Goldoftas & Attorney David Brown
Thousands of children in California are left without a guardian because their parents have died, abandoned them or are unable to care for them. *The Guardianship Book* provides step-by-step instructions and the forms needed to obtain a legal guardianship without a lawyer.
California 1st Ed. $19.95

how to modify and collect child support in california
Attorneys Matthews, Siegel & Willis
California has established landmark new standards in setting and collecting child support. Payments must now be based on both objective need standards and the parents' combined income. Using this book, custodial parents can determine if they are entitled to higher child support payments and can implement the procedures to obtain that support.
California 2nd Ed. $17.95

a legal guide for lesbian and gay couples
Attorneys Curry & Clifford
A Legal Guide contains crucial information on the special problems facing lesbians and gay men with children, civil rights legislation, and medical/legal issues.
National 5th Ed. $17.95

how to adopt your stepchild in california
Frank Zagone & Mary Randolph
For many families that include stepchildren, adoption is a satisfying way to guarantee the family a solid legal footing. This book provides sample forms and complete step-by-step instructions for completing a simple uncontested adoption by a stepparent.
California 3rd Ed. $19.95

how to copyright software
Attorney M.J. Salone
Copyrighting is the best protection for any software. This book explains how to get a copyright and what a copyright can protect.
National 2nd Ed. $24.95

the inventor's notebook
Fred Grissom & Attorney David Pressman
The best protection for your patent is adequate records. The Inventor's Notebook provides forms, instructions, references to relevant areas of patent law, a bibliography of legal and non-legal aids, and more. It helps you document the activities that are normally part of successful independent inventing.
National 1st Ed. $19.95

legal care for your software
Attorneys Daniel Remer & Stephen Elias
If you write programs you intend to sell, or work for a software house that pays you for programming, you should buy this book. If you are a freelance programmer doing software development, you should buy this book.—Interface
This step-by-step guide for computer software writers covers copyright laws, trade secret protection, contracts, license agreements, trademarks, patents and more.
National 3rd Ed. $29.95

patent it yourself
Attorney David Pressman
You've invented something, or you're working on it, or you're planning to start...Patent It Yourself offers help in evaluating patentability, marketability and the protective documentation you should have. If you file your own patent application using this book, you can save from $1500 to $3500.
National 2nd Ed. $29.95

SELF-HELP LAW BOOKS & SOFTWARE

ORDER FORM

Quantity	Title	Unit Price	Total

Sales Tax (CA residents only):

7%   Alameda, Contra Costa, San Diego, San
        Mateo & Santa Clara counties
6 1/2% Fresno, Inyo, LA, Sacramento, San Benito,
        San Francisco & Santa Cruz counties
6%   All others

Subtotal _____

Sales Tax _____

TOTAL _____

Method of Payment:

☐ Check enclosed

☐ VISA   ☐ Mastercard

Acct #_____ Exp._____

Signature_____

Phone (   )_____

Ship to:

Name _____

Address_____

_____

Mail to:

**NOLO PRESS
950 Parker Street
Berkeley CA 94710**

**For faster service, use your credit card and
our toll-free numbers:**

Monday-Friday 8-5 Pacific Time

US   1-800-992-6656

CA   (outside 415 area)   1-800-445-6656

      (inside 415 area)   1-415-549-1976

General Information   1-415-549-1976

Prices subject to change

Please allow 1-2 weeks for delivery

Delivery is by UPS; no P.O. boxes, please

ORDER DIRECT AND WE PAY POSTAGE & HANDLING!